BIRMINGHAM LIVES
Through Children's Eyes

BIRMINGHAM LIVES
Through Children's Eyes

Ed. MARCUS BELBEN
with Ann Heath and Bridget Roe

BREWIN BOOKS

First published by
Brewin Books Ltd, 56 Alcester Road,
Studley, Warwickshire B80 7LG in 2004
www.brewinbooks.com

ISBN 1 85858 253 9

A cataloguing in Publication Record
for this title is available from the British Library.

Typeset in Times
Printed in Great Britain by
Warwick Printing Company Limited.

ACKNOWLEDGEMENTS

I would like to thank the following for their support, assistance, information and images:

Billesley Primary School
Birmingham Central Library
Birmingham Evening Mail
Birmingham Post
Brookmeadow Court Sheltered Housing
Chinnbrook House Sheltered Housing
Hall Green Library
www.virtualbrum.co.uk
Yardley Wood Library
Yardley Wood Local History Group

Liz Collins, Billesley Primary School and all the volunteers were excellent in providing support and any help required to run the project.

Most importantly I thank all the participants, whose hard work and dedication has produced such an impressive project. This book is a tribute to you.

Marcus Belben - Projects Co-ordinator
Birmingham Lives

This Project has been funded by:

Local Heritage *initiative*

Marcus Belben

FOREWORD

I believe that my grandmother grew the best rhubarb in Wolverhampton. It grew like Leylandii. It could easily have offended the neighbours because of its size. The reason her rhubarb got so big was not that she lived close to a nuclear power station, but because of the way she tended it. She looked after it better than she looked after my grandfather. Onto that rhubarb went every pot of tea leaves, every out-of-date apple, every spadeful of manure speedily salvaged from the road, after the rag-and-bone-man (or, more accurately, his horse) had passed through. There was strong competition from the neighbourhood rose growers for this treasure-trove.

Chris Upton with Iris, Tasha and Tanya, opening the exhibition at Birmingham Central Library.

Every so often, up would come one of those sticks and I would be given an egg-cup of sugar to eat it with. It was a treat to compare with a lump of butter rolled in sugar, or a spoonful of condensed milk. And whilst I was chomping through the rhubarb, watching the strings get longer and longer, she would remember things and tell me.

She would recall the first time my grandad took her out on what we would now call a date, but was then called 'courting'. He took her to a picture-house - the Queen's probably. My grandfather was a forgetful man, even in his youth. He would have made a good absent-minded professor had he been educated beyond the age of 13. So the film ends, the National Anthem is played and my grandfather heads off for the last bus home, having entirely forgotten that he took anyone with him.

Even thirty years later I could sense the feeling with which my grandmother recalled the long and solitary walk home to Whitmore Reans.

There were lots of other tales too, but I was too busy wrestling with those long strings of rhubarb to recall them.

We all remember. Some of us remember better what we did in 1956 than what we did yesterday. But memory is an act of co-operation. It works best when there is someone to talk and someone to listen. It's what we do best and yet what we do least. But I can't think of a better way of making history live than talking to someone who lived it.

The official name for this activity is oral history, and over the last few years we've begun to recognize how much everyday history is locked away in people's memories, the kind of history you would look for in vain in books and documents.

With support from the Local Heritage initiative, funded by Heritage Lottery Fund and Nationwide Building Society, Birmingham Lives' AGElink project has put together the young and the old and set them talking to each other. Questions and answers; curiosity and experience. You only have to read these stories and look at the photographs to see how rewarding this experience can be for both sides of the conversation. For the children in particular it is a chance to see, not how history comes alive, but is already alive and well and living in Birmingham.

And all without a single stick of rhubarb.

Gisela Stuart MP (second left), with Chris Upton (top right) and project participants at the exhibition opening at Birmingham Central Library.

Dr Chris Upton
Newman College of Higher Education

CONTENTS

1. Introduction   1

2. Activities   4

3. Group Discussion   11

4. Life Stories   19

5. Other Stories   74

6. Student Views   122

7. News & Views   124

*For Doris and Jock who died before
completion of this project and for Arthur,
who was born during this project.*

Thank you Tim and Nikki too.

1. INTRODUCTION

In the summer of 2000, a handful of community art workers got together to work on the Birmingham Lives 2001 Project (some of the stories of which are included at the back of this book). This was to be the beginning of a number of projects, based around the life stories of older people living in Birmingham.

Billesley AGElink project is part of a wider AGElink project involving four schools, residential and nursing homes, sheltered houses, the local library services and countless older people living in South Birmingham. The AGElink project aimed to bring together young and old who may live locally, but have no contact with each other.

Students from Billesley Primary School worked with older people living in Brookmeadow Court and Chinnbrook House Sheltered Housing, as well as members of the Yardley Wood Local History Group. They used video, voice recordings, photography, art and crafts, and the written word to record interviews with the residents. The students also record their thoughts on the people they have talked to, where they live, what they did and what they thought of the project.

The stories were exhibited locally, and then joined the other AGElink stories in Birmingham Central Library for a larger exhibition in the Centre for the Child over the summer of 2003. This book is a record of their work.

I am particularly proud of this book. It represents a year's worth of hard work from over fifty people aged seven to one hundred.

BILLESLEY PRIMARY SCHOOL

Billesley Primary School is an inclusive school with 476 pupils aged three to eleven, from Nursery through to year six. This project has given children who attend our Cadbury Time Children's Club the opportunity to make valuable links with local elderly people. The Club, which was set up in 1995 for Parents/Carers who work, or were returning to study, offers before and after school care and school holidays activities.

Everyone, including our volunteers, staff and children, works hard together and we look for ways in which we are able to give back to our community. Being a part of this project is not just about helping us cover the community links area of our Quality Assurance programme. The project has been so successful, it has led to our club receiving an award from Birmingham Childcare Network for innovation and excellence. But most importantly, the project has led to closer ties and friendships between individuals and the Homes, which is already leading to more activities and projects involving Billesley Primary School and Billesley residents working together.

Liz Collins - Community Development Officer
Billesley Primary School

The AGElink project has been a wonderful opportunity for all those who took part. The friendships which developed, as young and old discovered each other, made the time spent away from the classroom doubly valuable. Skills were rediscovered and taught, and an appreciation of the worth of age and youth, were developed by all.

The exhibition that came into school provided everyone in the school community with a fascinating insight into life in Birmingham not so long ago. We heard laughter and remembrances as adults visiting school discussed what they saw.

How important projects like this one are to help us to learn to live together, to appreciate everyone's experiences and to bring our communities back together!

Jan Millington - Head Teacher
Billesley Primary School

BIRMINGHAM LIVES

Birmingham Lives is a community arts organisation dedicated to celebrating the lives of older people. We work with care homes, day centres, libraries, schools and voluntary sector organisations interested in older people living in Birmingham.

Much of our work involves workshops within care homes teaching computer skills, arts and crafts and creative writing. Our work encourages participants to recognise the value of their skills and experiences. Through the workshops and other projects, like AGElink, we seek a greater understanding, integration, and respect of older people within their own local community.

PROJECT WORKERS

Marcus Belben, B.Eng, M.Sc, M.A.
For the past seven years I have worked in care homes for older people in Birmingham, as a community art worker. I also work with special needs groups, adult education, the youth probation services and I am a part-time youth worker.

Ann Heath, B.A., M.A. (arch ad)
For the past few years I have been pursuing a career as a writer; this book is one of my first publications. Before this, I was a professional archivist in Manchester and Sheffield.

Bridget Roe, B.A., RGN
I am an experienced NHS nurse, with a special interest in the care of older people. I am also a graduate of Birmingham University, with a degree in English Literature.

PROJECT CONTRIBUTORS

Christopher Heath, Daniel Green, Laura Eccles, Marie Vinge, Monisha Chauhan, Nicole Jones, Nisha Parmar, Peter Wood, Saffron Scott-Reed, Signe Vinge, Tasha Beck, Tanya Beck, Tanya Collett, Thomas Barrett, Townsend Forbes. Barry, David, Dorris, Elsie, Flos, Howard, Iris, Jock, Joyce, Joyce, Katy, Margaret, Mary, Mrs Gibson, Peter, Sheila, Stan, Una, Una.

PREVIOUS PUBLICATIONS

Home is where the Art is, Marcus Belben, Full Potential Arts, 1998
Looking in from the outside: Community Art and Art Education, Marcus Belben, In Art Education Discourses Vol. 2, ed. Jacquie Swift, ARTicle Press, 1999
Rembrandt's Late self-portraits: Images of Aging, Marcus Belben, in The International Journal of Aging and Human Development, 2000(1)
A Part of our Lives, ed. Marcus Belben, IKON, 2001

2. ACTIVITIES

Artwork – Inspired by the stories

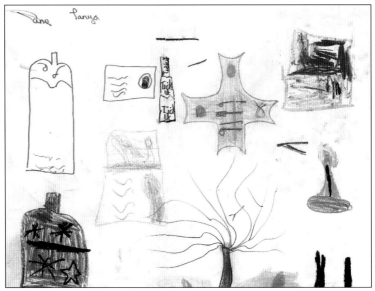

Artwork – Inspired by the stories

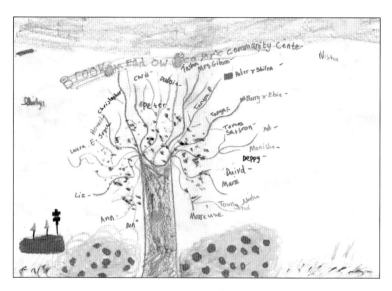

Cakes, recipes & potions

We used old recipes, some taken from Margaret's mother's recipe book (see pictures), and had a coffee morning to sample the results!

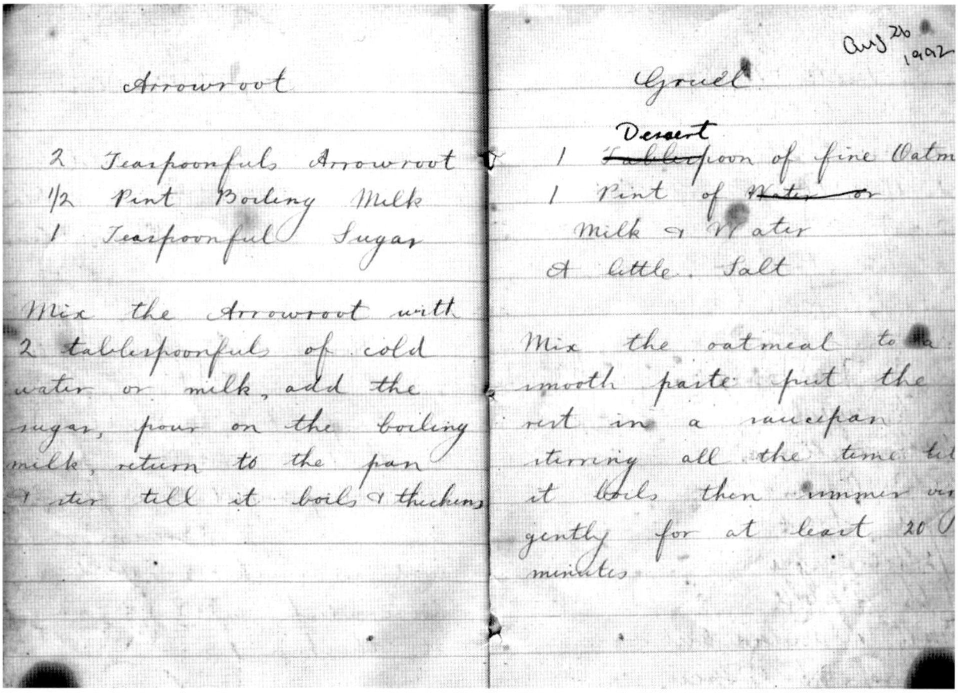

Arrowroot

2 Teaspoonfuls Arrowroot
1/2 Pint Boiling Milk
1 Teaspoonful Sugar

Mix the Arrowroot with 2 tablespoonfuls of cold water or milk, add the sugar, pour on the boiling milk, return to the pan & stir till it boils & thickens

Aug 26 1992

Gruel

1 ~~Tablespoon~~ Dessert spoon of fine Oatm
1 Pint of ~~Water~~ or
Milk & Water
A little Salt

Mix the oatmeal to a smooth paste put the rest in a saucepan stirring all the time till it boils then simmer ver gently for at least 20 minutes

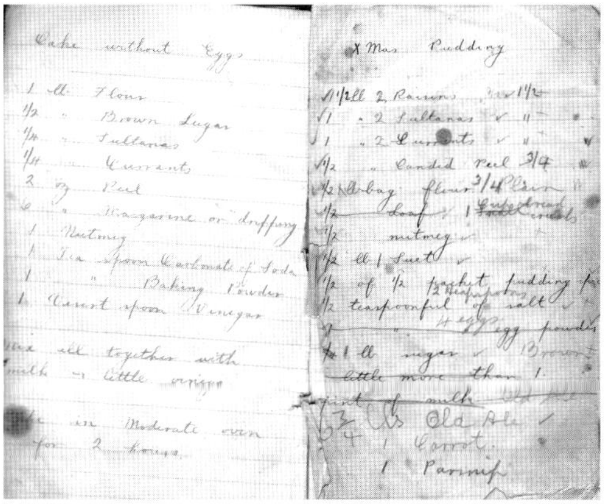

Cake without Eggs

1 lb Flour
1/2 " Brown Sugar
1/4 " Sultanas
1/4 " Currants
2 oz Peel
6 " Margarine or dripping
1 Nutmeg
1 Tea spoon Carbonate of Soda
1 " Baking Powder
1 Desert spoon Vinegar

Mix all together with milk & little vinegar

Bake in Moderate oven for 2 hours.

X Mas Pudding

1 1/2 lb 2 Raisins 1 1/2
1 " 2 Sultanas "
1 " 2 Currants "
1/2 " Candied Peel 3/4
1/2 lb bag flour 3/4 Plain
1/2 loaf 1 ~~stale~~ Cup bread crumbs
1/2 nutmeg
1/2 lb Suet
1/2 of 1/2 packet pudding spice
1/2 teaspoonful of salt 1/2 teaspoon
~~" egg powder~~ 4 eggs
1 lb sugar Brown
~~little more than 1 pint of milk~~
3/4 lbs Old Ale
1 Carrot
1 Parsnip

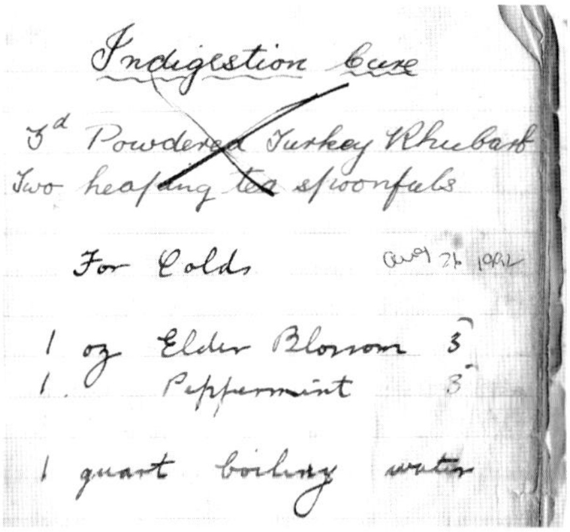

Indigestion Cure

~~3d Powdered Turkey Rhubarb~~
~~Two heaping tea spoonfuls~~

For Colds Aug 26 1992

1 oz Elder Blossom 3
1 " Peppermint 3

1 quart boiling water

Everyday objects from the past

Participants brought in objects from the past the children would find interesting, from old tram tickets to radios, clothes pegs to pop bottles.

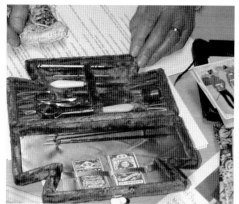

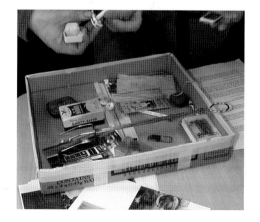

Pompoms, rag rugs and wool roses

The group worked together using a number of traditional knitting crafts, including corking, pompoms, rag rugs, wool roses, peg dolls and other knitted objects. We used wool, rags, scrap material, pegs, bodgers or prodders (a sharpened wooden clothes peg), and bobbins (four nails hammered into wooden cotton reel)

3. GROUP DISCUSSION

Games

(Peter) My wife, Sheila and I, before the War, when we were about eight, we used to live about ten houses away from each other. I was a very naughty boy in those days and I used to throw stones at the girls, Sheila particularly. One of the things Sheila used to do was put on shows in her garden shed, dancing. We used to go to look at them. We had to pay to go in with white stones.

Can you tell me any other things about when you were young?

(Pat) When I was your age? I had a friend called Pat, and unfortunately she was quite a plump girl. She always used to get caught eating. When I'm called Pat, it's not my first name. My first name is Beryl. I use my second name, but at school I was always called Beryl. Her name was Pat and she used to be called Fat, but then children are unkind, don't you find?

I lived in a cul-de-sac. We all knew each other, all the boys and girls of the same age. We used to play in the road. In those days not many people had cars so it was safe. You'd have seasons for things. You'd have a skipping season. Do you skip?

Yes.

We also had something called the whip and top. Peter and Sheila will remember. We used to draw hopscotch. Do you play hopscotch?

Yes. What sort of games did you play (to the others)?

(Margaret) We used to play all sorts of things. We had our whip and top, and we'd colour the top with all different colour chalks so it went Whoo! Round and round like that! And I had a dolly and a dolls pram. We used to play ball up against the wall, and hopscotch. What do you play?

Sometimes we play tig, and hide-and-seek, and we play football.

Margaret: Oh, we didn't play football. Not the girls, anyway. That's changed now, though. One of the women I know here, her granddaughter's in a rugby team!

11

(Peter) We played the same sort of games, really. We used to play hopscotch on the pavement, because there weren't any cars, really. We used to roller-skate, on the road. One of the roads, not far away, was tarmaced, so you could roller skate there. But we only had one pair of roller-skates between the six of us, so we'd have to share them.

We used to collect bus numbers. That may seem strange to you, but that was one of our hobbies. The bus route where I lived, the number eight, it's still there; it used to take one hour to go around. We used to get the bus numbers, and wait around an hour until you saw it again. And then you used to see how many times you could see it in a day. It was a silly game, really, but that was one of the things we used to play.

We used to play hide and seek. Again, because we used to live in a road where there were a lot of children, so there were a lot of us, lots of friends. In the same road there was four or five girls, but we didn't play with the girls much. We used to play boys games, cricket, and things like that. We used to play cricket in the street.

One of the things was the horses. The bread man used to come with his horse, and the milkman, the coalman, and two horses used to come to deliver the beer. So there were horses everywhere. That was the way people got around.

What games did you play?

(Barry) Like Peter, I played Hopscotch and Whip and top. We also played Marbles. Because in the street, there were cobbles, it was ideal. There were lots of holes to drop the marbles into. So that's where we used to play.

(Pat) Do you remember the ice cream man used to come round on Sundays? She used to ring a bell and shout, "Stop me and buy one!" She was on a bicycle. There was a big box on the front where she kept the ice cream.

My Dad used to say, "There you are, here's sixpence". You used to take a basin to the ice cream man and you'd have the basin full for sixpence – that's two and a half pence.

Did you get treats if you were good?

(Margaret) Oh, yes, when I was about 5 or 6 my Mum and the lady next door used to go shopping on Saturday morning and leave us kids in the houses and when they came back they used to bring us all a cream horn back. Do you know what a cream horn is? It's a cake with flaky pastry like a cornet and cream at the end. Lovely. Then we had sweets, as well, like Jelly babies and Aniseed balls, but not many because we didn't get much pocket money at all.

Did you have any toys when you were younger?

(Pat) Yes. I had a big doll. One year my sister, who is three years younger than me, we got a doll each. It had a china head, but then its body was a sort of papier-mâché thing. I've still got my doll, except the arms and legs have fallen off. They were attached with a piece of elastic inside. Over the years its rotted away, but I've still got the doll. It's got no eyelashes, because I remember pulling them out, and it had teeth, which were pushed in.

   We both had this doll, exactly the same, and she went racing across the road, to show her friend the doll. She fell down the steps and smashed the doll's head. This was Christmas morning. She always thinks I was so horrible because I wouldn't let her have my doll. But I thought, why should I let her? She'd broken hers – it wasn't my fault.

She'd probably break yours next.

I've still got mine. My mother wanted a doll very, very badly. She was one of six children, and they hadn't got a lot of money. All they ever got for Christmas was a stocking with an orange, a few sweets, a brand new penny and a lump of coal. The lump of coal was for each child to light the fire on Christmas morning. But she wanted a doll, and they all had a little gift as well, and she got her doll.

   She was so disgusted when she got her present. It was about eight inches tall, and it was made of wax – just a little wax doll. When she sat by the fire – she was always being told off because she sat too near the fire, the doll began to melt. She was so disgusted with it, she took it out onto the road, and out onto the tramline. She waited for the number 33 to run the doll over. She got much enjoyment watching that doll getting smashed.

What did you get for Christmas when you were little?

(Margaret) We always had an orange and an apple in our stocking and a new penny! That was a big thing then. We had other little things, like dressing up dolls, and I used to have a pot farmyard as well, with all the animals and a mirror for the pool, and fences, it was lovely! My Mum and Dad would stay up late on Christmas Eve, getting the presents ready and making all the mince pies. One year my brother Dennis was so excited he woke up at one o'clock in the morning and went to see if Father Christmas had been yet, and he finds Mum and Dad with all his presents, but they hadn't even been to bed yet!

Houses

What are Back-to-back houses?

(Peter) The back-to-back housing was different in Leeds to how they are in Birmingham. They were literally back-to-back. There were no backyards. The back of one house backed onto the back of the other in the next street.

So if your friend lived on the other street, it would be good if you could have a door so you could go through and say, "Hello!"
 You had to go around to the next street, but the toilets were outside, in the street.

Uh! That's disgusting!

You had four houses and then the toilets were in a little square before the next house. In some ways, fortunately, ours was the nearest house to the toilets, so we didn't have to walk all the way down the street. It was terrible in the winter.
 Of course, in these streets, we hung the washing. Outside the door, across the street, all the way down the street, there were lines of washing. The line was low and you had a block to push it up, so the horse and carts could get through
 (Sheila) I used to live in back-to-back housing. Every so often there was an entry to a little courtyard, and there would be another six houses in the courtyard, and in the middle there was what we called the brew house. There were two of those, and they were where the women did the washing. We had a big copper boiler inside, and a little fire below, we used to light to boil the water. There was one tap and a trough.
 We used to fill buckets with cold water from the trough, carry it across the yard and pour it into the big boilers. These were kept going nearly all the week, because every mom had their day to do the washing. It was a top up system and keep stoking the fire. Everything used to go on the fire, even potato peelings.
 We used to do the washing in the big boiler, then fetched out with a stick and put into a tub. Cleaned with clean water, washed, gone through the big mangle and then hung on the line. If it was your day and it was pouring down with rain, heaven help you, because it was hard luck. You had to do two loads of washing the next time you used the boiler.

What's a mangle?

It was a cast iron frame with two big wooden rollers, and a big handle on the side. You'd turn the handle around and water used to come out of the clothes and back into the tub.

(Peter) It was instead of a spin dryer. Spin dryers hadn't been invented then.

(Sheila) There was a blue block in a muslin bag, and that was always put in with the water, and that made the water blue. It was for all the white clothes to be put through, to make the whites even whiter. Men's collars were starched, so you had starch.

(Pat) My Mum, when she first got married, she starched the whole of his shirt – it came out like a board!

School

Did you go to School?

Barry: Yes, five days a week!

Did you have fun at School?

Barry: Fun? Some of the time, yes. I can still remember playtime at 11:00. All the mothers used to come up. It was a very tight knit community. All the mothers used to come up and push food through the railing for the children.

Why did they do that?

Barry: To feed us.

Did you get told off at School?

Peter: I tell you what - we used to have the cane at my school. I had a brother who was very naughty who was the year above me, and because he was always having the cane, my name became synonymous with his. Very often I'd get the cane because of him. I was well behaved because I was frightened to be naughty.

I had the cane once on the hand. The teacher called me out. I'd burned my hand the day before. I'd picked up a red hot poker. I'd got blisters on all my fingers, across there. The teacher called me out and said, "Put your hand out, Peter."

Four strokes was what I was going to get. I said, "I'm sorry miss, you can't hit my hand because I've burned it", being cheeky.

So you know what she said? "You've got two hands, Peter. Put the other one out."

So she gave me four on my good hand, and then she gave me four more for being silly and picking up a red hot poker!

You were naughty at school you got told off there, and hit, and when you got home you got another smacking off your Mum for being naughty at school.

The men teachers – we didn't have many because they went off for the war, but the men teachers used to bang you on the ear so hard that your ears used to sing for ten minutes afterwards. But we were very good, because if you weren't, you'd be caned, and if you were very bad, you'd be caned by the Headmaster in front of the whole school. But it was rare, because you really didn't want the cane. I only had it once the whole time I was at school.

They used to have the slipper as well. They used to throw things at us as well. Do you still have chalkboard cleaners? Wooden things with a soft side? Well they used to throw that at us. And they were very accurate. And they used to throw chalk. One lad got hit in the eye, he had to go see the nurse. He came back with a pad on his eye, and the teacher told him he better not do it again or he'll get the other eye.

We used to have detention as well. School ended at four o'clock, so we had to stop until five o'clock. Sometimes you had several, and if you hadn't done your homework, sometimes you had to do your homework, or write lines.

I was very lucky, you had to go to room fourteen for detention. It so happened my classroom was room fourteen. So when I was on detention I didn't have to leave my own desk. When the teacher came in, they asked if you had something to do. I used to tell lies and say, "Yes, Miss, I've got something to do."

I'd open up my desk and get my homework out. But they soon found out about that, and they'd move you around, or change classroom, and not let you open the desks.

We also had things called, 'Long Tots'. They were like giant sums to add up and take away. A book full of sums, and it had numbers with six digits. We used to have to add them up, and if at the end of the night you got them right, you could go home. The teacher had the answer book. We never got them right because they were so huge. But someone found out you could get the answer book from town, so we bought an answer book, and we all had the answers passed around so we could go early. But then they got suspicious and they said, "Nobody can add up these numbers in three minutes and get them right!"

That didn't last very long.

Travel

What's a tram line?

There was one that went up to the Lickey Hills, and you could sit outside, and your ambition, really, was to sit outside. It was quite nice outside. It used to go all the way to the Lickeys. It was a very popular route. It used to go all the way up the Bristol Road.

It cost me two pence, which is equivalent to less than a penny. And you'd get a bottle of pop for that. The shop that you'd get that from…When you go down to town on the bus, when you go past the big Midland Red bus depot in town, the shop that used to sell those was next to there. We used to go swimming, at school, to Kent Street Baths. Because I used to go on the bus, they used to give us a little plastic token. You'd get red ones for a penny, green ones for a penny ha'penny. This is old money. You gave this to the tram or bus conductor like a pass. You took it on the bus.

When we used to come out of the baths, we used to walk across, to catch the bus back to school, like you do, with our little tickets. We'd go right up the road, and buy ourselves some ginger pop, drink it quick at the tram stop then take the bottle back and get a ha'penny back for the bottle. We'd go back on the tram burping all the way back to school.

Next door to this shop was a shop that sold meat pies. You know the ones you get at the chip shop? Well these weren't quite like that. These were little squares, six whole pence, they were; Boiling hot and full of gravy – no meat. Not much anyway, and all this hot gravy used to come out. That was after we went swimming.

When you drank the pop, did the marble…

Yes, it stopped the pop coming out. When you pour the pop into a glass, you do it that way. When you want to stop it up, you do it that way. Nothing comes out then. They're very crafty

How did the marble get in there?

Good question!

When I was at school, because the war was on, you couldn't get paper. You used one of these. You got a wet cloth and wiped it off. Now, I'll write Peter; that's me. Get a cloth and rub it off. Its slate, and that's slate as well.

Do you know what these are? Pegs these are. Have you seen these sort. Gypsies used to make them and sell them door to door. They'd sell the pegs and then they'd say, "Can I tell your fortune?" - Because they used to say they can tell fortunes.

"Cross my palm with silver."

If you said, "No, go away", they used to chalk on your front door, to curse you.

They used to say that'll put a curse on you. You'll have bad luck. We used to go around and rub them off again, or, I shouldn't say this, but we'd go around some of the old ladies. We'd play them up and put a chalk mark on their door. When we saw them, we'd say, "Mrs. So-and-so, the Gypsies have been. We'll rub the chalk off your door for a penny!"

You've seen that sort of peg? But, what the girls used to do is make them into little dolls.

Oh yes, they've got little heads, haven't they?

Yes, that's the head. Those are pipe cleaners to make the arms, and then, if you look inside, that's the peg, and there's the dress. Little peg ladies, and the girls used to make them.

Elsie: We used to call the pegs dolly pegs, but I don't know which came first, the peg name or the dolls.

Peter: What my mother used to do, when the gypsies used to come, because a lot of the ladies were frightened of gypsies, because they were frightened they'd put a curse on them... She used to say, "I tell you what. I'll tell your fortune."

They'd say, "No, no!" and they'd run off because they were frightened my mother was a witch.

4. LIFE STORIES

Barry and Elsie

Did you have a nice house?

Elsie: Yes, lovely. I had four brothers, all older than me, so I was the baby. As a girl I was very spoilt, by my Dad, in particular. When I was three we moved into a big housing estate, on Bordesley Green East. It had freshly been built, so it was all new – Alston Road, Corbyn Road, Denville Crescent, Norton Crescent, Mead Crescent, where my friend still lives today, and Caldwell Road, were all one big estate.

Barry and Elsie with Tom, Saffron and Nisha.

My old friend on Norton Crescent used to live next door to me. She was a very dear friend, who is still a dear friend after seventy-five years. We went to school together. She had a baby, and when her husband was killed in the war, I helped her with her baby. The Christmas when she was expecting her first baby, the telegram came to say her husband had been shot down over Germany. He never had a father, but he had two wonderful silly mothers!

We go every week to take her shopping, and she's like me, but a bit older, so I say to her, "You're older than me". She's six weeks older than me. So yes, it was very happy. We played in the street and we played all those games.

When we were old enough we went to the pictures. You couldn't get into the pictures unless an adult took you. We used to stand outside and say to people, which you wouldn't do these days because it wouldn't be safe, "Would you take us in please".

It would be two pence, and we'd give the people our money and they would take us in the pictures, and then you could sit where you liked. As you got a little older you'd buy some lipstick and powder, and we used to make our faces up, and we used to go dancing to the local dance, which was up in Stetchford.

There was Heartlands Hospital, which was then Little Bromwich Fever Hospital, and you could see the children on the balconies outside, because they had tuberculosis or fever, and these sorts of things.

It's a huge place now, but when we lived there it was a tiny fever hospital. You could see the children on the beds. I bought a house that backed onto the playing fields where you could see the hospital. They were out on the beds overnight, quite a few hours. I never saw them come in. If they had tuberculosis they had to be outside. That was the treatment then. Of course it is different now.

All the surrounding area has changed completely. Saltley Grammar School was in the same area. The school's the same and it's still going strong, but not as a Grammar School.

Do you have any family?

Elsie: Yes, I have a daughter, Susan, who lives in Spain. She married a Spaniard. I have a son who lives in Bromsgrove, and he's got three sons.

My son is a P.E. teacher and my daughter was a teacher. When she went to Spain she taught in Spain as well.

Two of my brothers, Reg and Dick – Well, their Father died in 1917, and their mother brought them up, until she died in 1921, leaving the two boys. Rather than have them go to a Home, my mother took to them, and a fortnight later had my younger brother, and a year later had me. They were in the house before I was born, and were brought up as my brothers, always.

This is my father, right in the front row (sixth from left), in the First World War. And he was in the bomb throwing squad. He looks a bit cheeky, and he was a bit. Almost in the middle there, with a cigarette in his mouth, which I hope you're all against these days.

The one regret in my life, Dick said to Barry just before he died: "If only she'd let us call her Mother." She said no, they had a mother, and she was their aunt. They always called her Auntie. All their lives, which was sad in a way. You don't hear things like that. You can't hear children saying 'Auntie'. People have always said, and it was said at her funeral, if it hadn't been for my mother they would have been in an orphanage and brought up as orphans. Instead of that they had a loving home.

The only way I learned that they weren't my brothers, was somebody at school once said, "They're not you're Brothers, because they've got a different name to you". I went home crying, because I didn't know. My mother explained they weren't my brothers, but they were treated as brothers. If there was one treat in the house, it was divided into five.

And this was my brother in India during the Second World War.

Elsie and family at the Queen's Coronation party.

I used to say my parents were the most wonderful people, and if my children were as happy as I was as a child, I would have been a good Mum.

A school called Alston Junior School held a party for the Queen's Coronation. They had a big party in 1953, when she came to the throne. We were all there. My two children, my son and my daughter, are both there. They are all dressed up. They're all dressed for school. It's the same school I went to. It's still there today, you know.

Barry: There were seven brothers and sisters came out of Russia at the turn of the century. They stopped off in England to go to America. Six of them eventually went to America. My Grandfather was the only one who stayed here. It must have been 1904 or 1905. My Dad's eldest Sister was born over there in 1903, and my Dad was born over here in 1906.

Were any of your family in the war?

Barry: Yes. My Dad was in the army during the war.

That's my Dad and that's me and that's my sister *(Below)*. He was in the army then the Second World War. We saw quite a bit of him during the war. He didn't go abroad. An uncle of mine, mum's brother was in the war. He was in the air force. He was in Singapore when the Japanese took Singapore. He was captured, and, as a Japanese Prisoner of War, he was transported to another island in the Pacific somewhere. The ship was attacked by, I think, American warplanes. They thought it was a Japanese warship, and sunk it. He was killed. I was too young to remember, of course.

Elsie: My four brothers were all in the forces during the Second World War. One was in North Africa, one was in India, one was in Northern Ireland, the one that really wanted to do the fighting, and the other was out after a few weeks, because he was in a lorry when there was some gas escaping. He went in quite healthy, and came out with epileptic fits. There was no compensation for that. So they all served their time during the war. They were all away for the time of the war.

Norma with her Dad and Sister.

We revisited that spot two years ago, where this photo was taken in 1939. That's us on the motorbike belonging to their son.

Now this again, is my brother, who at the time was in the Church Army. This was prior him going to North Africa. He later became a vicar.

Register showing Barry and Norma's evacuation.

Barry: I was talking about the war. If I can just digress a little. On Tuesday, 29th August 1939, I was seven. My Mum said to me, "On Sunday you can have a party".

I said, "Oh, Good!"

But we didn't get that far, because on the Friday, 1st September, I was evacuated. The War started on Sunday 3rd September. The children in the cities, for safety, were taken out of

A day's outing at Keighley.

the cities. I went to a little village in Lincolnshire. We started school on the 18th September, and then we came back on the 17th November.

The school I was at in Leeds was one big building separated into two. In one half was the boys and in the other, the girls. There was one playground surrounding the school with railings between the two, so the boys and the girls were completely separated. You could talk through the railings. The boys were evacuated to one area, and the girls another.

I went with the girls, so that my eldest sister could look after me. She was nine and I was seven. But she wasn't happy being away, so we came back fairly quickly.

Low Rail at Quarry Hills Flats.

We had one school trip a year. This picture is taken in Keighley *(Above)*. It was a day's outing. It was the only one I went on. It was the only one that was offered! It was once a year for the top class, 'standard eight'. You got to there then you left. It was hiking, rambling, looking at plants, and falling into brooks and streams and that sort of thing.

And that was my Mum at school – Fourth from the left on the middle row *(Above Opposite)*. Third from the right on the middle row is her sister, my Aunt. Of course, this was in Leeds.

I was nine and a half when we moved to Quarry Hill flats. Prior to that I had lived in various houses, including a back-to-back.

Quarry Hill was various big buildings, but we called each entrance a block. It was down this path *(Left)*. There was this low rail.

Cross Stamford Street School.
Barry's Mother, fourth from the left, middle row.

It was amazing on a summer evening; You could see all these people from the flats sat on those rails just chatting. There was a playground in the middle. There were three playgrounds, because the blocks had different areas.

It was just a spare bit of land, but this was one of those play areas. This picture was of the annual Quarry Hill carnival. They had a parade, they had a carnival queen, with attendants.

Now these are four beauty queens *(Below)*, and this was me and my friend with them. This was the carnival in 1951. They were the first four.

They had so many put themselves forward and they had a panel of judges decide who the carnival queen was going to be a couple of months before. She'd parade around the flats and crowned. Usually she'd go round in an old banger of a car, although one year they had a new model from Austin, and it was quite flash.

They had other different competitions too. My younger sister won the fancy dress competition one year. She went as 'The Gainsborough Lady'. She won the cup for that!

The four beauty queens with Norma and her friend.

I was in the RAF here, on the day before my nineteenth birthday, and we were singing 'Hang on the Bell Nellie'.

That's me on Ladywell Walk *(Below)*. It's just off Hurst Street, where the Chinese Quarter is now. On the other side are the back-to-back houses that they're renovating on the corner.

There was a big Jewish community in Leeds. Although there were more Jewish people in Manchester, there was a higher percentage in Leeds.

I did meet anti-semitism as a kid. I remember one day in particular. Two of us were waiting for a bus to go from School. We must have been about twelve. A group of four lads set upon us, and fortunately a bus came before it got too far.

Barry and friends singing 'Hang on the Bell Nellie'.

Barry on Ladywell Walk.

We were able to get away on the bus. There was definitely anti-semitism then. That was during the war, of course.

I don't personally come across it now. I think it has got better for us. It's still around, of course, but it's not quite as bad as it was. I don't think it's diminished, but there are different target groups.

Elsie: On the radio it was talking about racism and Muslims. There seems to be a cry against them. Basically they were saying they want to take over, and make our country, or Birmingham, I suppose, into their type of religious country. They were saying that was wrong because the percentage is quite small, but it does seem at times that we've got a lot of mosques. But there are Synagogues, and I am Church of England. I don't go to church regularly, but I am a Christian, and Barry takes his religion seriously.

26

Above: Young Norma.
Right: Young Barry.
Below: On their Front Doorstep.
Below Right: Barry and Norma.

David

My Mum was my Dad's second wife. They moved here with six children, four from his first marriage and two from theirs, plus his sister, Ada, who was deaf and dumb. Then they had two more children, my brother and myself, the youngest.

Dad died when I was eleven months old, leaving Mum with eight children and Aunt Ada to look after. The three eldest soon left, though, and I can't remember them ever living with us.

David meeting the group.

Mum worked in the canteen at Harvo, the bakers in Watery Lane, Bordesley, where they made malt loaf and a ginger cake called Ovro. I remember she brought us dried fruit from the work, which we couldn't afford otherwise. We also used the butchers near there, so if ever she was off work ill, which wasn't often, one of us had to traipse all the way over to get the weekend meat.

My aunt had come to stay with us because she had nowhere to live. She looked after us kids while Mum went to work and we adopted our own sign language to communicate. Like, one of my brothers broke his arm, so he was always this (strokes arm). I was the youngest so I was always baby (mimes cradling). And woe betide anybody who set on us outside. All the kids round here would roam around and fight and all sorts, but she'd always defend us. She was built like an ox! Eventually she went into a home, when she got quite old.

Until I was eleven, I went to school at Billesley. Then I got a scholarship to Moseley Grammar. I didn't take full advantage of that, unfortunately. I regretted it later, but I used to stay off school with my older brother, and Mum wasn't there to make sure we went. So I ended up in the top class back at Billesley, until I left at fourteen.

I ended up working in Research and Development at Bakelite. We tried to improve the products or find cheaper ways to produce them before the factories made large numbers of them. The works arranged day continuation, where you could study one day a week, and I started night school, as well, but I just never did the work. I started playing table tennis and that was more important! When I got called up, I still had no qualifications.

I went into the forces in 1948, due to "duration of present emergencies" after the War. National Service came later. First I was sent near Liverpool, for "square-bashing", where they knock you into shape. It was all about doing everything as fast as possible, and getting the discipline right. The sergeant was always yelling at you. I've seen blokes harder than me in tears! And you learn very quickly not to get the first bed in a billet, because the corporal would always pick on the first man he saw!

There was one chap there, older than the rest, who'd been in the navy, and, while we were shaking in our boots, he didn't go on parade the whole eight weeks. One day, he stayed in bed with "toothache" and the sergeant told him to report sick and have it out! So, to get out of parade, he had to lose a tooth!

After six or eight weeks of that, I went into the air force as a technician. It was a waste of time. There were three levels of technician; fitter, with a year's training, mechanic, with twenty weeks, and assistant, with only eight weeks training. I was a Radar assistant. Well, you can't learn much in eight weeks. I was mainly at Middle Wallop, Hampshire, at a control and reporting school where officers were trained to direct fighters. My only job was to keep a mobile generator full of diesel and start it every day!

I found the air force a bit of a surprise! Living round here, I'd learnt to swear early on, though not as early as the kids today, I have to say! But most of the people in my billets were ex-grammar school, or even ex-public school people who had just done their A-levels and were waiting to go to university. They didn't swear at all, so I stuck out like a sore thumb! I went into the forces and actually stopped swearing, whereas most people went in and started!

After twenty-one months, I came back to live here. At first, there was my Mum and the four younger children: Violet the eldest, Wally, John and me.

Round here, it wasn't unusual to have six kids at home even with the older kids working. You didn't leave until you married. There was less freedom of movement, and, of course, it was rare for kids to go to university. I only knew one local lad who went on a scholarship. He did very well, learnt Russian and ended up as a director of Nestles.

My auntie had left, and the other children had married, though we kept in contact with the youngest, since he married a local lady. He got a bit

David sharing a joke with his new friend.

toffee-nosed and wouldn't bring his lady to our house! He had worked on the Lucas shop floor, but after marrying into her family, he went into insurance, and ended up as the School Board man, checking on truants.

Being in the forces with all those qualified people made me realise table tennis wasn't exactly a living. So I went back to Bakelite and decided to get qualified. By this time, you only got a day off for learning if you were already on a course. I had to take evening classes three or four nights a week for an ONC in chemistry. It took me four years with all the practical work as well, and it covered physics, chemistry (inorganic and an introduction to organic) and maths. I went on for another two to get my HNC, then a Diploma in Plastics Technology, and eventually an Associateship of the Plastics Institute.

This was all on top of a full time job, five and a half day, forty eight hour week. I'd work eight till half past five with a half hour lunch, then bike it to Aston Technical College, for up to three hours study. It was a bit much really! Four or five of us from Bakelite started off going but only two of us finished the HNC.

It helped get me promoted from the works to the staff, a drop in salary, but you got other perks like paid sick leave. Otherwise, any sick pay came from the benefits agency after five days off, and nothing before that. When I first worked, I got seven hapenny an hour - about thirty bob for a forty-eight hour week. I never earned more than £10,000 a year, and that was not even technical work, but pharmacy stores and invoicing at Selly Oak and Dudley Road hospitals until I retired. By then, I'd moved because of the job shortage – you had to take what you could get.

Working so much, you lose some of your social contacts. I still managed to play for South Birmingham Table Tennis Club one night a week. I'd race in from class at nine or later, play two quick games and then go home. We had to ask the other teams if they minded me coming late, otherwise they could have just claimed my two games as forfeit. There was only one occasion when I had to step down because a friend on the opposing team warned me his captain was planning to claim them. The club was run by Adrian and Doris Haydon, both champions. Their daughter, Ann Haydon, was a world champion. I remember her when she first started. She wasn't big enough to play, so she used to stand on a platform to reach. A few years later she started playing tennis, and she ended up winning Wimbledon. You may know her as Ann Jones.

My other big interest was big band music. Then, the American bands would come to Birmingham town hall, Duke Ellington, Count Bassey, Ella Fitzgerald. And before I went into the forces, I went to the local hop at the community hall, which is now the Sure Start Centre at the bottom of Trittiford and Chinnbrook.

The DJ would be there every week with two turntables for 45s and LPs, playing foxtrots and so. I still go to see big bands now - MYJO, the Midlands Youth Jazz Orchestra, and another called Fatchops. They're both excellent. They've won the

BBC Big Band competition and everything. I don't really understand how these kids get into it.

It isn't even their parent's music - that would be The Beatles.

Anyway, Violet married in 1953, and went to live with her half-sister. It didn't work out, so she came back, with her husband and child. It was the early 1950s and housing was very scarce. There were three lads in one room, Violet and her family in

The Chinnbrook Centre.

another, and my Mum on her own in the other. My brother Wally was seriously ill. He'd a swimming accident while I was in the forces, and they found he had epilepsy and a brain tumour, but most of the time he was with us rather than in hospital.

Violet only managed to get away with her young family because Wally was so ill, and that was after John got married and left in about 1957. Wally by that time had a caliper on his leg, and he'd lost his sight and a little bit of thought power. He'd wake up in the night and not be able to tell you what he wanted. He died soon after. So then it was me and Mum. She died about fifteen years ago.

She had a long and very hard life, particularly early on. I got the best of it, really, being the youngest. Life got a bit better, a bit easier, as the older kids started earning.

I've lived around here all my life. I've seen the area change. I grew up with loads of kids my age, then they married and moved out, and for a while there were many neighbours without children, and now there's kids again. There's less discipline now, though. Parents think, "My kids won't have to do what I had to do", and so there's been a lessening of discipline all along the line, until it gets to proportions, which to me are just unacceptable. It's a general malaise, I think. It's alright round here at the moment. The kids are really young and lively, and the police have helped.

It's been fun doing this project with the kids, too. It's been a surprise to me how interested they are, really. And of course, I've had a lot of fun getting my tip cat out, and my whip and top. I've enjoyed the time I've spent with them a lot.

If the area's changed, I'm told I haven't changed much though! My niece did a presentation for my 70th birthday, all photos of me from eight upwards and I look the same! I even met a couple at the library who swore they knew me, and they recognised me because I used to rent a garage off them. In the late fifties!

Howard and Joyce

Signe: When were you born?

This is a long way back! 8 June
1918, just at the end of the First
World War. I'm eighty-four,
now. And do you know who
wants to be eighty-four? Anyone
who's eighty-three, that's who!

Tanya: Do you have any family?

I'm married to Joyce, and we
have two daughters, Jane and
Lesley. And I have a brother
called Leonard, who is two
years older than me.

Howard gives the children the thumbs up!

Tanya: Which schools did you go to?

Well, Loxton Street Primary School, and then the Central Secondary School in
Suffolk Street. The areas have been redeveloped, and both the schools I went to
have been knocked down. I think its personal!

Tanya: What did you like at school?

I loved rugby football, table tennis, cricket, and games like that. I wasn't so keen
on athletics. In class, I liked languages and maths, and calculus.

Signe: Even without calculators?

Yes, even without calculators!

Signe: Did you have a library in your school, or a book fair?

Yes, we were always able to borrow books, but we had to buy our own textbooks.

Tanya: Did you have homework after school?

Every night. And you never forgot it because you'd get punished, with lines or sometimes the cane. Normally, if you did something wrong, the teacher would simply tell you to hold out your hand and whop! Once, twice, three times. But if you'd been really bad, the whole school would be brought together in the hall; the head teacher would take the cane, bend you over a chair and whack you six times. That was about the worst thing that could happen.

Nicole: Did you get the cane?

Yes, I had it once or twice. Very painful it was too!

Signe: Can you remember your teachers' names?

Oh, I remember one called was Llewellyn Cuthbert Evans – he was very Welsh – and he signed his name LC Evans. We always called him Elsie!

Tanya: What did you do at lunchtime?

We stayed in school, because we had no way to get home, no cars or anything. We had to walk there and back, so we took sandwiches to eat in a big room, and then we'd go out into the playground and play.

Nicole: What do you remember most from being young?

I think you remember things that are important to you at the time. I remember starting my new school. I remember my grandfather's funeral, when we went to the cemetery to see saw him buried. Happy things as well, of course. Christmas parties, and the like.

I remember when new things came out, the first gramophones and motorcars. Telephones, too. I was eighteen before I used one of them! We had no TVs, and only a few radios.

Tanya: What was your favourite song?

I always liked the lamplight one, Lily Marlene, but luckily for you I can't remember it properly!

Nicole: Did you have a favourite singer, you know, like Tom Jones?

Yeah, Max Bygraves.

Nicole: Who?

No one seems to know him now! I went to buy a Max Bygraves record and asked the young man at the counter in Virgin and he'd never heard of him either!

Peter: Did you buy the Beatles records?

I quite like some of them but I don't particularly like loud modern music.

Peter: I like rock.

Now see, that's far too noisy for me.

Nicole: What did you do in the War?

I joined the army before it started, and when war was declared, there was little action for a long time. We went to France in 1940, but I was taken prisoner by the Germans, and I spent the war in a Polish prison camp.

Nicole: How did they capture you?

There were three or four of us stuck in the middle of France, with the Germans advancing really quickly. I'd lost my gun – it was useless anyway, because I had only had five bullets with it – and we were dodging the Germans, stealing eggs from farms to eat. You put a hole in them at both ends and suck the egg out raw. One day, I broke into a farm but there were Germans there. I just saw a German soldier pointing his rifle at me, and that was it. I was captured and sent to Poland.

Nicole: What did you do there? Were you working?

Yes. Digging mostly, long trenches for pipes and so on. We unloaded coal, too, a lot of really nasty, dirty jobs. We didn't get much food for it, either, and they didn't even pay us!

Nicole: Was it very hot and dirty?

No, in Poland, it's very cold. You had to move about to keep warm. You worked to keep warm.

Tanya: Did you escape, or did they let you go?

You couldn't escape. There was nowhere to go. Poland was an occupied country, so the Germans had simply taken everything over, and the Poles couldn't help us. Then the camp had bars and barbed wire all around it. We used to say it was there to keep the women away!

Nicole: Did the Germans hurt you?

Well, yes, they were nasty. If you were too naughty, you could be shot.

Nicole: What was the camp like?

I was in one camp for a long time, with nine hundred prisoners, all going out to work everyday, all very unhappy. It was a fort built by the French when Napoleon went into Russia, a round building, with a circular space in the middle, and originally a moat full of water. We slept in rooms crowded with three tier bunks that reached right to the ceiling, on mattresses called palliasses, packed with straw.

Tanya: How did you get out of Poland?

When the war was finishing, the Germans knew they were losing, so they took us out of Poland and made us march towards Germany. Then, one night, the front line of our troops passed by us, and suddenly we were free. Just like that!

Nicole: Did your Mum miss you after being away for the whole War?

Oh yes, when I came home, my Mum hadn't seen me for five years. When I was first captured, it was a long time before I could let her know I was alive. The War Office just said I was missing. Then the Germans let me send a postcard home. When Mum saw it lying on the mat, she just knew, by instinct, that it was from me. She was shouting, "He's alive! He's alive!"

Nicole: Was your wife scared that you got captured?

I didn't have a wife then. Joyce was a friend of my sister-in-law, and after the first twelve months, she started writing to me. She wrote to me for four years, but obviously we never actually met until the war was over. And when we finally met, we ended up married! We have been married now for 55 years. We just had our emerald anniversary.

Tanya: After the War, did you have another job?

Yes, I started to work in a bank. And do you know, when I was a very little lad, I had an auntie who read teacups. Do you know what that means? When you had a cup of tea in those days you always left tealeaves at the bottom of the cup. Well, my auntie would turn the cup upside down, and read the pictures she saw in the tealeaves, to tell your future.

Tanya: Yeah, they have that in Harry Potter.

Well, this aunt told me that I would go away for a long time, but that when I came back home, I would then have lots and lots of money going through my hands. So everything came true.

Of course, I wanted it to be my money, not someone else's!

Howard and Joyce.

Iris

What food did you eat?

Homegrown, mostly, or we would get farm produce.   Sometimes it was quite difficult.

Did you go to the park on your own?

No, we were at school, mostly. We did sometimes, but we were never allowed to pick flowers. There weren't that many about. buttercups and daisies, and bluebells. You could go in the park and make daisy chains.

What was your home like?

I had two sisters, and our mother used to make sandwiches, not proper sandwiches, but bread and lard. It was very nice actually. It was called rosemary lard, and we had a bottle of water. We didn't drink tea and coffee or anything when we were little children. We drank water. We didn't have many toys, but we had what we used to call season games, you know, skipping, or hopscotch or whip and top. Some of the boys used to get buttons, and you would skim them to see if you could hit another button.

There was a game called kellum where you threw a ball at the wall. I had a best friend called Isobel. We used to share our secrets, and little stories. We didn't go to the cinema much, so we didn't have a favourite film.

Did you play board games?

You used to have one called skittles. I remember playing it one Christmas time, where you had to see how many skittles you could knock down.

At Christmas you'd have a stocking with an apple and a penny in the toe, and one present, a little doll or whatever, that's all we had. We'd make decorations with paper, coloured paper. You wouldn't like to live in those days.

Iris gets on well with the children

Oh I remember the ice cream man, we called him Italian Joe, he used to stand under the same lamp post every Sunday, and you'd go and fill up a jug or a basin.

Did you have books?

Not like they are today. You would have one for Christmas.

Did you enjoy school?

I was a naughty girl at school, I was talking to my friends when I shouldn't have done, and I got the cane. You would get it on your open hand. You would get slapped a lot, as well. I don't think it hurt us. They don't do it now. Perhaps they should.

Did you have a school uniform?

No you didn't have it then, but you'd have a singlet and knickers to play P T.

Did you have new clothes?

Well, you used to get hand-me-downs, if you'd got an older sister, and you'd get hers as she grew out of them. The next one down would have what you were wearing. There were three sisters in our family.

We used to do our washing in what you'd call the brewhouse. You'd go up an entrance, into the yard where there used to be the brewhouse, where your mother would do the washing. She'd light the fire under the copper, fill it with water (there wasn't any hot water) and have a tub with a pole called the maid. She used to bang all the clothes in the tub, and put them through a great big wringer, not too hard, of course.

Was it scary in the war?

Ooh yes, very. There used to be a shelter in the garden. They used to come along with pieces of steel, and your dad or your uncle used to dig a big hole, a very big hole, and build up the sides and put the steel on it. No door, just an old curtain. You could hear the bombs go all round you.

What if it hit on the top?

Well, you'd die, but they didn't go for the little shelters in the garden. They didn't aim for those. They aimed for big buildings, mostly. Sometimes, if a bomb had dropped nearby, the water would go off, and they'd put what they called a standpipe in the road and you'd fetch water from it. They used to have incendiary bombs, and if they dropped some of those, the place would catch fire.

Do you know what an ARP warden was?

Well they used to come round when the sirens went off and check you were safe. Occasionally, they'd lose their life.

Did you have any food in the shelter?

Sometimes we'd have sandwiches. Sometimes you'd come straight home from work and go straight down the shelter, and be there all night. The floors were damp, and the walls. You'd have your coat on.

Iris and friends.

Katy

My mother came from quite a big Catholic family. She had at least six sisters. Her family had a little shop in town where they sold bits of everything. One of her sisters, May, was a suffragette. She went off to London, and we barely saw her. All the other aunts we saw now and again. I remember they had a piano, and they could all play and sing, there was always a great carry on there.

Dad was a hand polisher on the cars at Wolseley, you know, a really good job, but he never really kept his family properly. And I was the eldest of ten children. I was born in 1909 at Tower Road, and the rest were born in Devon Street, Saltley, near the big gas cylinders.

I was five when the First World War broke out. I can remember when the zeps came over, and we were watching one go right over us. My mother was worried to death because if they'd

Katy helping out with the drinks.

dropped a bomb on the gas cylinders, we'd have been flattened! Dad was sent to Ireland, and my mother got an allowance off Wolseley. That's when she found out how much money he was getting! Suddenly, we were ever so well off.

We all had new clothes and boots, and Mum had our photograph taken all together. I've tried to find it since, but it's gone.

But nothing really changed after the War. We only had two bedrooms for all of us, one living room and one cold water tap. We lived in a big terrace of about fourteen houses, with a shared brew house, which was a big boiler where everyone did their washing one day a week. We had a coal fire to cook on, and candles for light.

Friday nights were bath nights. My mother filled the big washing tub, and baby went first, followed by another and another! And we used to go to the public baths and have a wash there. You got soap and towel and everything.

As the oldest, I helped Mum with the younger children. When I was eight, I was first up to light the fire and boil the kettle to make Dad's cup of tea before he went to work. Later, me and my two brothers all worked to earn half a crown a week each. That seven and six kept us mostly. Dad's wage just went to the pub. We'd buy some bacon and render it down, and that would feed the lot of us.

I was paid to scrub the convent steps before I went to school, and polish all the convent cutlery on a Saturday morning. Even then, if I was late, I still had to kneel in front of the whole school, and have the cane! Everyone did who was late, no excuses.

Every month, as well, the head teacher checked your writing, and if it wasn't good enough, you got the cane. Mine never came up to par. I was an excellent speller, I just couldn't write neatly.

We had good teaching really. It wasn't a convent school, though some of the teachers were nuns. We did mental arithmetic, doing sums in your head. That I was good at! Now they use calculators all the time.

I loved reading too. I'd read anything. I can even remember saying "I love reading my deep books," not knowing what I was talking about. We used to go to the Vauxhall Library, near Saltley Road. It's a listed building now. Whenever I go past it now, I can see myself at sixteen, standing there reading a book. I used to quite happily leave the pram outside with three children in it while I went in and read. You couldn't do that now!

We were never bored. There was too much to do. The church used to have dances for the boys and girls, or we would walk to the parks and spend hours outside with all sorts of games, like hop scotch.

We all left school at fourteen. My eldest brother got into grammar school, and the teacher came and begged Dad to let him go, but Dad refused, burnt the certificate in front of him! My brother still did really well, becoming Head Engineer at his works, and working for the government in India and Africa. Two brothers went into accountancy and even my youngest brother, who'd been a devil for school and always played the wag, went to Australia

Katy's Auntie Gladys.

41

and became a town clerk and a magistrate. We've all been a credit to the family, so you can do it if you want.

When I was fourteen, Mum needed me to earn money, so, through a neighbour, she got me a millinery job. She didn't really know what it was, though. It was seasonal work, and all the girls were higher class than me, girls who didn't really need the money. They could never get over me. When I first turned up, they said I'd looked the same that way as that way, because I had no shape, no curves! So the girls made me some proper underwear. My Mum must have thought I was suddenly growing on top!

I couldn't believe my luck. I loved it there, rather than having the kids to look after, and I used to play up a bit! The seamstress was a very old lady who sat at the top of the room, and she made me sit with her, I was such a play about. She said, "You must be the only one!" And I said "What! There's nine more of us at home!" I really enjoyed my life then.

When that work finished, I had to find another job. I've had that many. Some of the girls would work six months and then have a break, but I had to work all the time.

Then, in 1936, I lost my sister, Eleanor, to TB. My Dad had had it, and one of my brother's had been away to a fever hospital with it. But I was devastated by her death, and I just couldn't go back to the work I had been doing. So I went to work

Lourdes 1939. Tom's brother is in the middle, holding up the canopy.

in a doctor's house in Willenhall, somewhere completely different.

It was a great big house, with so much wood that needed polishing, and the cook had me cleaning the Aga every day, on my knees. On top of that, I had to work in the doctor's surgery. I lost pounds in the first week. I gradually got worse, until the doctor, knowing there was TB in the family, got me properly checked out. They found the problem was a tiny extra rib, only five eighths of an inch long, near my neck that was affecting me, so they had to operate. The operation impaired my hand – it took eight months of special exercises to recover and I've had pain in my arm ever since.

Katy's Brother in Navy uniform.

When I was better, I went to work for this lady, who was expecting her second baby – she had a little boy already. She paid me two pounds a week, a lot of money in those days. Unfortunately, she lost the baby, but we were all so upset, I stayed to help. Her husband was a captain in the admiralty, from a strong Methodist family. Still, they sent their son to St Agnes Convent School, because it had such a good name. Of course, I was still Catholic, and he always thought I was teaching his son all the Catholic prayers and that, rather than the nuns!

Anyway, the lady had another baby, but she had to have it privately rather than at home, because they had money. She had to go back into hospital because of some problems, so I had to look after the baby, and then nurse her when she came out too. They got me a beautiful silver tray to say thank you, but I've lost it now.

I got engaged just before the Second World War. His name was Tom, and I'd known him for years, since he was in our church football team, and Mum washed the kit. He'd asked me to go with him before, but I still wanted my freedom. Then, in 1939, we all went to Lourdes, with Tom's brother, who had worked to become a priest since he was fourteen. It made me realise I had to make something of myself.

I decided I wanted a family. So I agreed to go with Tom, and soon he asked me to marry him. I think I said, "Yes, you fool!" My brother George couldn't believe it. "All that time," he said, "you'd have nothing to do with him, and now you're going to marry him!"

Then war broke out. Dennis and Victor went into the Navy, and Margaret went into the Wrens. Fred was the first to get called up. He was in the army as a Sapper. He injured his ankle in France, so they sent him as a trainer to Dover for the rest of the War. Tom was in a reserved occupation, engineering, so he wasn't called up. Still, we barely saw each other. He was in the armed guard at night, and I was doing factory work during the day, and doing nights with the Nursing Reserve.

I was good at nursing. Once, when a doctor was training us, he asked us what to do if someone was badly burned. I'd just come in the door and said it straight out without thinking. He said, "That's the girl I want working with me, if she keeps quiet!" I nursed over in Erdington, at the mental hospital there, where some of the soldiers came.

The factory was very different. We had to wear overalls, trousers and all. There were only two of us girls who had to, on the whole of the factory floor. And then they found out I was Catholic – the things they said to me! Communist things! I ended up a booking clerk.

I remember we lived in an area where a smoke screen was put up, to protect the airframe factory, Nuffield's from bombing raids. The soldiers would set off these smoke canisters all along the path, and then half the time, they'd come in, have a bath and go off to a dance somewhere, while we had to put all sorts of wet cloths up to the windows to try stopping the smoke!

Finally, we got married and I had to stop work, because I became ever so sick with my first baby. The doctor had to give them a note, though, they were very strict about working at that time, we all had to. We ended moving to a new house in Pype Hayes, with three bedrooms and a bathroom. I couldn't get over it!

I've got three girls – Mary, the eldest, in London, Katharine, who lives in Queensland, Australia, and Theresa, who lived in Tasmania but went to New Zealand. And I have a foster son, Christopher. Theresa used to work in a nursery home, and Christopher was there as a baby. We used to bring him home for the weekend, and I carried on after Theresa went to Australia. He used to cry so when I left him that day, I wrote to the home offering to foster him fully, and they agreed. He's got children now, closer to me than my own grandchildren, because he lives in Northfield rather than Australia!

Katy relaxing in the sun!

44

Margaret

Nicole: When were you born?

September 12th 1923.

Tanya: Where did you live?

Alum Rock, and we moved when I was seven to Warstock, Prince of Wales Lane, until I moved out in 1965.

Signe: Did you have any brothers and sisters?

Yes, I had two brothers, Jack and Dennis. When we were growing up, I was the baby of the family, so they used to play me up. They put things in the bed, like holly and

Margaret with Peter and Nisha.

deckchairs! Mom would tell them off, but they'd take no notice. "It was only a joke, Mom"! And if anything had to be carried I carried it! We'd play cricket in Daisy Farm Park, and I always ended up carrying the wickets and everything! I was the muggins!

Peter: Did you have any cousins?

Ooh, lots of cousins.

Peter: Cos I've got about two hundred thousand of them!

Signe: What was your home like when you were small?

In Alum Rock? I thought it was nice. A home is what you make it wherever you live, isn't it. It was an old house. You came off the pavement straight into the front room. There wasn't a hallway or anything, and the stairs went off the living room, as we called it, and we had three bedrooms. We didn't have a bathroom or anything then, just a tin bath in front of the fire. We had a little yard, with a passage that served about six houses, and a garden beyond that. Prince of Wales Lane was very different, with a bathroom and everything.

Nicole: Did you have to help round the house as well?

We all had our jobs to do. Dennis had to clean the boiler, and Jack had to clean the bathroom and I had to do the hall. I helped with washing too. We had a tub and a wooden pole – a maid – that you bounced up and down on the clothes. Then you'd put them through the wooden ringer, empty the tub in the drain outside and put clean water in to rinse them all, before putting them on the line.

Margaret's old Grammar School photo.

Tanya: How did you do your hair?

I used to get my hair singed rather than cut. They used to do it with a taper, you know, comb it down a long way and then singe it short.

Tanya: What was the name of your school?

Which one? I went to lots of schools, the infants at Anthony Road School, Alum Rock until I was seven, then Yardley Wood Juniors until eleven, and finally Waverley Grammar School.

Signe: Did you like school?

It was alright. I don't remember the infants much, but my Mum said I cried on the first day because they made me hold hands with a boy. And I didn't like the knickers! They were cotton with awful lace round the edge that I used to tuck up my leg.

Signe: Have you got any old photos?

Only a long one of my grammar school. That's the whole school there. It was a mixed school, so there was boys and girls, and that's me at the back. We always had to wear school uniform. The headmaster, head mistress and teachers are in the middle in their gown, like a black cloak, can you see? That was about 1937, so I'd have been fifteen.

Tanya: What lessons did you like?

I learnt French and German, and the usual Maths, Literature, Art. I liked French and Art as well, not that I was very good at it! I liked the Maths teacher, he was Mr Gibson and the French teacher, Mrs Griffiths I think.

Tanya: How did you get punished at school when you were naughty?

Well, we had to write lines, a hundred lines… "I must not do this.."

Tanya: When we're really good in class, we're given marbles. We have a white board, with a line down the middle, one side happy, one side sad, and if you're bad you go on the sad side.

Nisha: What did you do at playtime?

Ooh, all sorts of things. When I was a little one like you, we used to play with our whip and top. We'd colour the top with all different colour chalks so it went Whoo! round and round like that!

Peter: So what else did you play with?

Well, I had a dolly and a dolls pram. I used to sew a lot and knit too, for as long as I can remember.

Tanya: I like doing that too, and crochet.

And we used to play ball up against the wall, and hopscotch. What do you play?

Signe: Sometimes we play tig, and hide-and-seek.

Peter: We play football.

Oh, we didn't. Not the girls, anyhow.

Peter: At our school, they play football. Nearly all of them.

In games, we used to play netball, and hockey, too. What about you?

Nisha: We're learning to play hockey, and basketball.

Peter: We play golf. I can putt a ball really well.

Signe: We do gym. Athletics.

Oh, we did that. We had a mounting horse to jump over, and wall bars, and a rope hung from the ceiling to climb up.

Margaret's sewing kit.

Peter: Cool. We've got a climbing frame, and monkey bars to swing along.

Nisha: Did you go swimming in school?

Yes, I went swimming when I was at Waverley. We went to Green Lane baths at Small Heath. I couldn't do it, though. They'd tie a rope round me and pull me along! Half the time I was sinking!

And then I've had some swimming lessons since I've been here and I still can't swim. We went to Fox Hollies Leisure Centre every Monday night to learn, but I've got something wrong with this leg, it just won't stay up. I can float OK, I just can't go anywhere. Can you all swim?

Nisha: Yes, from the deep end all the way to the shallow end.

Wood End near Earlswood reservoirs.
Thanks to www.virtualbrum.co.uk.

Tanya: Did you go on trips?

Yes, we went to Whipsnade zoo. And we used to go on nature study lessons down the Dingles or by train to Wood End near Earlswood reservoirs (Opposite Below).

Nicole: What did you do at lunchtime?

In junior school, I used to walk all the way home for my dinner and all the way back to school again.

Nicole: What did you eat?

Whatever was going, really; An apple, or occasionally a banana, with bread and butter. Things like chips weren't about so much then.

Tanya: Did you have any treats if you were good?

Oh, yes. When I was about five, I suppose, Mum and the lady next door went shopping on Saturday morning, and they'd bring all us kids a cream horn; It's like a cake with flaky pastry and cream in the end. Lovely! We had some sweets, like jelly babies and aniseed balls. Chocolate was a real treat. We didn't have much pocket money at all.

Peter: Yes. My Nan, when she was younger, only got two shillings.

Nisha: Did you have Christmas or Easter holiday?

Yes, but not as many as you! A month in summer and a week at Christmas and Easter. I was lucky because we always went away the last two weeks in August.

Nisha: What was Christmas like?

We decorated the house with paper chains, and a Christmas tree. We'd have a pillow case for present 'cos a sock isn't much good, really. Too small! Mum and Dad stayed up late Christmas Eve, getting the presents ready and making all the mince pies. We'd always get an orange, an apple and a new penny in a stocking. Then little things, like dressing up dolls. Once I got a pot farmyard, with animals and a mirror for the pool, and fences. Lovely! What do you want for Christmas?

Nicole: I want a Gameboy.

Oh we had nothing like that. TV wasn't even invented when I was young, and I didn't have one until after I was married. Dad used to have a crystal set - an old radio.

Nicole: When you were younger, what did you work as?

I was a wages operator on a machine. I'd work the pay roll out for the people to be paid out. In other words, I cooked the books! We had a nice crowd in the office. We used to have a lot of fun with them. I still work now - doing shopping for everybody else!

Tanya: Were you in the War?

Yes. I was in a reserved occupation because it helped the war, so I wasn't called up. I volunteered for the Red Cross. Do you know what that is?

Peter: I've heard of it. Its nursing, like an army thing, and if there's another war, they'll go and help.

That's it. I didn't nurse, though. I was on canteen duty at New Street station, serving tea to the troops in the middle of the night, or, when the doodlebug bombs came, the patients from London. Birmingham wasn't so bad as London for being bombed, you see. We'd go to the hospitals too, and made beds and served tea.

Nicole: Was it kind of scary?

Oh it could be very, very frightening. I worked in Handsworth, but the bus stopped at Ray Street and you had to walk right across to Snow Hill to get another one. That was scary. You didn't know where you were walking, and everywhere there was bomb mess. Still, you felt safer out at night then than now really. Everywhere

Margaret with family and friends.

Margaret tells the children all about the good times.

Margaret and her family.

was blacked out, but there were air raid wardens around and people helped each other more, really.

Bill, my husband, was in the Essex regiment and he was captured in Italy. They moved him to Germany on a cattle truck, but it was bombed and he got a hole in his head. They took him to a German hospital and treated him alright, then sent him to an officers' camp. The hole never really healed. Whenever he had a bad head, he blamed the War!

Signe: What did you do afterwards?

I only met Bill after the War, and we had one son, Steven. We went to live at Erdington in a high rise flat. We had a balcony that we could sit out on. It was lovely.

Mary

Thomas: What was the house like where you grew up?

I grew up in a two-up-two-down house in Putney, with a kitchen, a bathroom and toilet, and a laundry at the back of the house with a big sink in it. We only had cold water, though, we didn't get a water heater until I was about eight. We boiled water in saucepans or kettles, and for baths we had a big copper. We were lucky to have a bath and inside loo, but my mother had to pump water through from the washroom to the bath.

Mary with Townsend, Marie and Liz.

We had gas and electricity too, which was not all that usual. We also had a nice garden, not very big maybe but my Dad put down a lawn, and it had a small shed in it. As well as growing some ordinary salad vegetables, he had an allotment in which he grew all the vegetables for the house.

Where I lived, on one side was Barnes Common, on the other Richmond Park which is huge. I remember four huge houses there, massive places with twenty bedrooms! One was a seminary for Roman Catholic priests, one was a respite care home, like a holiday home for ill children and their parents, and one, The Rookery, had been a convalescent home for non-commissioned officers after the war and was eventually taken over by a business. One is now part of Froebel College, Surrey University. Three of them have been knocked down and tower blocks built.

Then there was also Wimbledon Common nearby. Do you remember the Wombles who wombled there?

Marie: I'm from Denmark, and they don't have them there.

Really, I've been to Copenhagen, and I've been to Helsinki.

Townsend: I'm going to Florida, and I'm going back to Jamaica. My Dad's Jamaican. My great great great grandma's grave is there, and all the people after her. There's a square of the Forbes family with all their graves there, and the path's a different colour so you know where to walk. It's really nice. When my Dad dies, he's going to be buried there. It's my inheritance, and I'm lucky because I'm the only heir.

It just shows how important your family heritage is!

Thomas: Did you have any brothers and sisters?

Yes, I had two brothers, but the middle one, Freddy, was tragically killed in a train crash in New Zealand. He was only twenty-six. It was awful, it happened on Christmas Eve 1953. I still have the eldest, Victor.

Thomas: Where were you at the time of the World War?

Well, I wasn't around in the First World War, but I knew a lot about it, because my father was heavily involved in the British Legion. I was a sea ranger and every year we sold programmes for the Remembrance Day service at the Albert Hall.

In the Second World War, 1939-1945, I was first of all at home, then the Blitz started and my whole school was evacuated to a place called Battle in East Sussex. Do you know Harold, the king who lost his eye in a battle? Well, that was the battle of Hastings, and we were in that area.

Then it got too dangerous. There were dog fights over the Weald and sometimes planes had to dump their ammunition and fuel so they wouldn't burn up if they crashed, so we were brought back to London. Then the buzz bombs started and I was sent to Seacroft near Leeds in Yorkshire.

Townsend: That was like The Lion, The Witch and The Wardrobe. They were sent away because of the war, too.

Do you know the Narnia books?

Tanya: Yes, I really like them.

Oh, yes, I may be older, but I do love them! I love books. They let your imagination open up. If you can read a good book, you can lose yourself from all your worry and care. It's a pity people don't read much any more.

Townsend: I like reading stories about things that could actually happen. Except now you'd never be evacuated like you were.

Well, it can happen again, you know. In Afghanistan, people have had to leave because of the war, and Kurds have had to leave Iraq. I had to leave my old home and move to Hertfordshire when I married, because the bombing caused such a housing shortage. I had to go to a job in a new town called Welwyn Garden City, and we got a council house in five months there, where I would have been waiting ten years in London. People still have to leave their homes for lots of different reasons, you see.

Townsend: But with our technology, a third world war will be worse than the First and Second put together.

Yes. Much worse. And I still remember the air raids at school, having to leave everything and go into the shelters. Very frightening.

Townsend: We're very lucky because so far only one person's been hurt in our army.

Well, yes, but a lot of other people have been hurt and killed, and we won't know the full toll until the war's ended. War is awful. In war, you have to attack the other side when maybe in peace time they would be your friends. What do you think?

Thomas: I don't think Tony Blair should be doing it. He's supposed to making the world a safer place.

You know, someone in the navy said to me, "I joined the armed forces for the defence of the realm, not to attack the defenceless".

Townsend: I don't like George Bush much.

Yes, and some people don't like Saddam Hussein. The problem is, if you are the leader of any empire, some people support you and some people do not, some consider you a dictator, others a leader. It is not an easy question at all. Saddam Hussein has been said to be cruel to his people, but then, we are never told the whole story. The first casualty in war is the truth. It's very difficult.

Townsend: Yes, George Bush is saying they did this and that, but they sold them some of their weapons.

That's right. They are in the World Trade organisation, and world trade will sell anything to anyone who's buying. Truth is the first thing to go in a war. All you get is misinformation, double meanings, all of that. I think it's really good that the children know enough to talk about it.

Did you hear the commander on the news at twelve today? He said "We are going in to capture...I mean liberate Baghdad." That says a lot!

Townsend: And they say this is going to stop the wars, but they know it's not, because there's going to be soldiers in other parts of the world and they're just going to fight again.

If you look at the world today, there's war in Lebanon, there's war in India, there's war between Tibet and China still, and Russia and China. They've just faded into the background, because this one has come to the fore. I have my suspicions about what will happen after this one too. Next question?

Tanya: Did you have any pets?

I don't now. I did when I was little. I had two rabbits. One was called Floppy Ears, because his ears hung down when they weren't meant to! At some time, they'd been broken. And I had a beautiful one who was completely black with a little white diamond on her head. She was a little darling.

We had dogs, too. One was a mongrel dog, that Mum and Dad would call a Heinz dog, because there were fifty seven varieties in him! We called him Ripper, because he ripped everything up. And we had a very nice big dog, called Beauty, like a St Bernard crossed with a retriever. I don't know what you'd call that. Dad had a huge ginger persian cat, but it went when I was only about eighteen months.

Then my brother had a tortoise once, with a hole in its shell. Someone must have dropped a stone on it. Dad would put plastic over its back to keep it warm in the winter, and he made a little coat for it out of document silk.

Dad brought most of them back with him. He was a great rescuer of animals. My Mum despaired. She used to say "Oh, no, not something else!"

Marie: What school did you go to?

I went to Huntingfield Road Infants and Junior, and Battle School, when I was evacuated. Then I got into Mayfield, a County Grammar School for Girls. In fact, in my year, there were thirty-four of us who won grammar school places, and we had three boys and one girl go to Christ's Hospital on scholarships. We weren't a brilliant year or anything, it was just a very good school.

We had Montesori teaching in the nursery and infants, which is child-centred, and we all turned out to be good at things like maths, music and languages. We had things like anti-bullying policies as well, really quite advanced. We were very fortunate. In my last year, the headmistress was Dame Margaret Miles, a well-known educationalist. It is still a girls only school, though now it's an ADT College. It had its 95th anniversary last year.

Marie: What games did you play there?

I played netball and hockey. They offered lacrosse, but I was no good at it, and in tennis, I could just about hit the ball over the net. I also did gymnastics and athletics.

Tanya: Oh, I love gymnastics!

I did too. Do you watch them?

Tanya: Yes!

And I used to run in athletics.

Tanya: We play football too.

Marie: Oh, I hate that!

Townsend: I like it. I'm a striker.

In gymnastics, can you do flip flops and hand stands?

Tanya: I can!

Townsend: I do break dancing. I can do a kick-up and a head spin. It used to be hard. It took me a year to learn ten moves at the beginning.

Oh, you are joking!

Tanya: What was your favourite game when you were young?

Probably hopscotch or skipping. We used to play with two balls, too, bouncing them under your legs. You really had to be agile. What's your favourite game?

Tanya: Gymnastics for me.

Marie: It would have to be tig or something. Because you get to run around. What was your first job?

I worked in the Almoner's department of Westminster Children's Hospital. The lady almoner is what you would now call a medical social worker. Then I went into medical records where I learnt to file and keep a well-organised system, and then I went to University College Hospital as a pre-training school probationer, like a student.

Westminster Children's Hospital medical workers team photo.
Mary is third from the left, bottom row.

Mrs Gibson

What School did you go to?

Vicarage Road, Aston. I left school at fourteen years of age. I didn't enjoy school. You had to do as you were told. They were very strict.

Did you have the cane?

Yes, I think we did, but only for the boys, not the girls. The girls just got their arms smacked very hard.

Mrs Gibson shows Townsend her photos.

What did the boys get the cane for?

Oh, only if they were very naughty. Bullying, or fighting, then they'd get the cane.

Do you have any special antiques from the past?

No, I don't think so. One thing I have got from when I was young, when it wasn't buses; it was trams. I've got a photo of the tram I used to travel on to go to Aston.

The Aston Tram Mrs Gibson travelled on.

What job did you do when you left school?

Well, first of all, when I left school, I went into a warehouse. When I was seventeen I worked in a cinema called The Hercules, on Rocky Lane at Aston Cross, where the Ansells Brewery was. I was working there until I was nineteen, and then the war started. My parents lived right in the middle of where a bomb was dropped. Just before that, my Father said to my Mother, "Let's make a nice cup of tea".

They hadn't been there ten minutes, when there was a tremendous blue flash, and everything collapsed. We had to live in one room, because the house might collapse completely, until we were moved.

What was it like in the war?

Well, very frightening. We used to have a blackout, which used to smell terrible. You weren't allowed a light on in the house. We had to have black curtains down, so no light would shine. The planes used to come over from Germany and they would drop bombs. If there was no light they'd just drop them anywhere. I can remember,

A young Mrs Gibson.

we had a shelter in the garden. We saw the house next door to my parents on fire, where an incendiary bomb had landed.

What lessons did you have?

Reading, writing, and arithmetic.

Did you have music?

Yes we had music, but it was old-fashioned music, not like today. Have you heard of Bing Crosby, 'Singing in the rain'? Very different to today. I like Bing Crosby and Fred Astaire.

Mrs Gibson shares the memories of her life with her young friends.

Did to university or college?

No, we didn't have the opportunity to do that in my day.

Did your Father go to War?

No. My eldest brother was a fire warden. He'd have the spades to dig the people out. It was very sad. I had cousins in the war. I had one in the Navy, never came back.

I go to church, and I'm a big Christian. I follow my parents, going to church. Do you go to Sunday school? Some of you do.

Did you have any children?

One daughter.

What did you do in your spare time?

I used to like to go to the pictures, because we used to have cinemas in those days. I had to be back in by nine, and not a minute after. If I didn't, I wouldn't be allowed out for a week.

Did you have tapes?

We had wirelesses, but they weren't like this (Pointing to a modern stereo cassette player). We didn't have many electrical things. Even in the streets there were only very small lamps. Not everywhere lit, like now.

Did you have Christmas trees?

We didn't have Christmas trees. People were so poor in those days they couldn't afford them. We'd have a turkey. They were very cheap before the war.

The Church of Ascension

The church I attend our Lord has 'Blessings to send'
To ones that attend of their own 'Free will'.
Thy spirit flows through our church 'Like a fire'
The hundred years that it's 'Stood'.
Our vicar we have 'The Sermon so strong'
One feels the power of God go through,
And the feeling of going to Church is good
To praise thy holy name. AMEN

Christ's Ascension
And a cloud received Him out of their sight.
No more the gentle hand will heal,
The quiet voice reply.
No more the sick and sad shall feel
The comfort of thy pitying eye.
By day we pierce not, nor by night
The cloud that veils thee from our sight.

But in common ways of men,
In market and in street,
Where little children play and when
The two or three together meet.
Saviour thy spirit still is there
To pity, Love and answer Prayer.
AMEN

Mrs Gibson

Peter

I can still remember my very first day at school. It was Cherrywood Road School, although we always approached it from Burbridge Road, off Bordesley Green Road.

Mom took me, all scrubbed neat, after the main starting time, and a teacher showed me where to hang my coat and I remember her showing me my peg, with an elephant on it, and telling me I must always use this peg, and remember the elephant. I also had a package of sandwiches, probably bread and dripping, wrapped in greaseproof paper. I can still remember

Peter with Tasha and Townsend.

those mushy, greaseproof-tasting pieces of bread. I also remember being told off by 'Miss', I think possibly on the first day. She wrote my name on the board, 'Peter', in large neat letters and then asked me if I knew any of the letters. I said, "Yes, Pee".

She said, "Oh No! That is 'P' for postman. 'P', 'P', 'P', never say 'Pee'!"

We always ate our lunch at playtime and went home to dinner, and either Mom, or more often, Grandad with little brother, Alan, would come to collect me from the playground and take me back at two o'clock. This was always an adventure because we had to go over the railway bridge on Bordesley Green Road, by Adderley Park Station, and granddad was a retired engine driver from Saltley Sheds, and seemed to know most of the drivers that were always shunting back and for the under the bridge. We used to wave if we had time, lean over the bridge and have a chat. He also knew the commissionaire on the main gates at Morris Commercial Car Factory, which we also passed.

In the afternoons often it was Mom, and we nearly always stopped to play on the slide and roundabouts on the recreation ground opposite the bottom of Burbridge Road. This is now an industrial estate – Cherrywood Industrial Park. The surface then was tarmac under the apparatus, and hard shale/ash everywhere else, and I can't remember any bones broken, or even being scratched or grazed. Nowadays soft rubber areas are provided, and great big guards either side of ladders and slides. I should mention that I did once have a suspected broken nose. It was my own fault. I was climbing up the slide the wrong way, and my brother, Alan, came down, feet first, the right way. He was wearing big hobnail boots, with 'horseshoes' on his heels. I think we had them from the 'Mail fund', for the poor and needy. He hit me squarely on the nose with obvious results – bleeding nose, lots of tears, and crowds of mothers and kids all around. Mom took me on the tram to the General Hospital, where a broken nose was not diagnosed. I just had black eyes, a big red nose and a good telling off for my troubles.

As I mentioned, my brother, Alan, joined me later at Cherrywood Road School, and I have a photograph showing him in the playground performing some sort of dance with his schoolmates. Also in this group in the same class is my future wife, some twenty years hence. I really only have two other vivid memories of this school before we were evacuated to Harvington, near Evesham. The first is staying over after school to see a magic show, and sitting on the floor of the hall eating my banana sandwiches, which mom had given me for tea. This was the last time I can remember having bananas until after the war. The other memory I have is of taking my model coronation coach and horse, all gold with white horses, and losing it at playtime. I remember the teacher coming with me all round the school to look for it, and me crying all the time, clutching the empty box.

As I said above, we evacuated to Harvington on the outbreak of war. I am certain that this must have been the Thursday or Friday before war was declared on the Sunday, because I remember the young girl of the house we were at rushing into the garden, crying, because her fiancé would have to go straight away into the army. We only stayed evacuated for a very short time because we were so homesick. I was eight and my brother seven. Mom had given us some paper and some envelopes to write to her, so we wrote, "Come and get us home!"

We hadn't got a stamp so we just put it in the little village postbox, and mom was there, 'hot-foot', and we came home. Of course, our school was closed, so we had to go to Anthony Road. Cherrywood Road School was taken over by Central Grammar School. I don't know if it was because they had been bombed, or if it was because their school was in the centre of town and was needed for some war effort. All sorts of buildings were being requisitioned for used by the Food Ministry, War Savings, A.R.P. etc. Anyway I remained at Anthony Road, despite the school being bombed at least twice, and for some time we had lessons in people's front rooms, usually teachers' houses. This might have been before going to Anthony Road, as an interim measure, because lots of schools were closed following the pupils being evacuated.

I don't really remember a great deal of life at Anthony Road, except being temporarily sent to Nansen Road, a girls' school then. When yet another bomb hit Anthony Road, I remember we used to save waste paper for victory, and this was collected and stored in the bombed part of the school. We were allowed one afternoon per week to go and help sort this into bundles. The Headmaster at the time was a Mr Brook, and I think there was also a Miss French. Most male teachers were away at the war at this time, of course.

I remember sitting the entrance exam for Saltley Grammar School. Now it's called the eleven plus. For weeks before, my dad and 'Uncle' Dick Barnett had us and his daughter working at night, doing test exams. I suppose they had got them from school and were trying to get us to do sums and English things that they couldn't do themselves. Mom would come to the rescue because she had stayed on at school until she was fourteen, so knew a lot more. Anyway, we must have passed because I got into Saltley Grammar School, and Brenda passed for Waverley Grammar School.

I started at Grammar School in September 1942, in the dark days of the war. My uniform was a grey cap with a badge on the front, a second-hand blazer, and short grey trousers. I think only the cap and tie were new. The rest were bought at the school by mom from 'Bring and Buy' sessions. Also, books were begged, borrowed or scrounged in the same way. My first days were rather frightening to say the least. All the bigger boys shouted after us, "Fag!" which I didn't understand at the time, and they kept chasing us and pinching our caps and satchels, if you'd got one. Our classroom was a wooden hut that replaced some that had been bombed and were supposed to be temporary. They are still there today!

I have lots of memories of Saltley – Being bombed out, having lessons in the cloakrooms, making model tanks on woodwork supposedly for orphanages, but we reckoned the teachers were selling them for Christmas. Game afternoons were one of the highlights of the week. I didn't really have any special skill at either rugby or cricket so, if possible, I'd get a letter from mom to say I had a cold or something. This got us off games, but all the sick and lame boys had to spend the afternoon pulling the big roller across the various pitches. The roller had shafts for a horse, but since we didn't have one, we were the next best thing. I think 'the invalids' were probably the fittest of the lot after a few weeks on the roller.

Running along side the school playing field was the main LMS railway line to London. Surprise, surprise, we all became train-spotters and spent our playtimes and dinner times, book and pencil in hand, on the bridge in Belchers Lane. I remember being caught on the bridge by the headmaster, Dr. Lloyd, one morning at about ten to nine. The bell went at quarter to, but there was an express, always pulled by a 'namer' that left New Street at quarter to. In order to see it and 'cop' its number, you had to risk being a few minutes late. On this morning, as Dr. Lloyd approached, we all remembered that a few days before, he had given the whole school a good talking to about boys wearing their school caps at all times, and being polite to people (He travelled home on the no.8 tram and often this was filled with shouting, cap-less boys). As he came up to us, red-faced and spluttering, we all quickly put on our caps and said, "Good morning, sir".

Unfortunately, this didn't seem to please him: he drove us all before him into the playground and called the prefect on duty to take our names and then all of us had to wait outside his study. When he appeared, his gown flapping behind him, he called us in, one by one, and gave us all a good roasting, and four detentions each, writing out, 4,000 times, 'I must not be sarcastic to members of staff and I must not congregate on the railway bridge, either before or during school hours.

I also had a similar punishment for 'Inundating the school playground'. I didn't know what this meant at the time, but I soon found out. It had been snowing and the snow had begun to thaw to slush. Some of us had decided to make a snow dam across the playground. We had hoped the slush would form a lake and make an excellent ice rink in the morning (the science lessons were sinking in, at last). Anyway, what we didn't know was that the deputy was watching us from the gym roof. The gym was below the level of the playground, and you can imagine the damage it would have done to the lovely polished oak floor. They would call this vandalism now, but we just hadn't given it a thought.

Suddenly there was a bellow from above, telling us, in no uncertain terms, to remain exactly where we were, and a gang of prefects were dispatched to take our names. This was a mistake on the deputy's part, Mr Cade, because although he knew our names, the prefects didn't, so their books were full of the 'swots' names in our classes. We all laughed, but not for long. A couple of days later, we were all standing in front of Mr Cade, trying to explain our little joke. The outcome was another four detentions.

I really didn't mind because my form room 14 happened to be the detention room. I just sat at my desk at ten past four, and as the duty detention teacher came in they always asked if we had been set any work, like lines or homework that had not been handed in on time. We, that is, our gang, always said we had and opened our books and got on with our homework for that night. If you hadn't got anything set, the teacher would hand out 'long tot' books. These were whole pages of six figure sums to add up. It didn't take long for one of us to find out that the answer book was available at 'The Midland Educational' in Town. We all collected some money together to buy one. I think it was 6d. After that it was passed from desk to desk, and we always got these vast sums correct, much to the surprise of the teachers.

Another really good part of the week in summer was swimming lessons. These were on Friday mornings at Kent Street Baths in 'Town'. Looking back on this time now remembering, I suppose it really was some of the best years of my life. I found the old programme for our prize giving the other day. Guess what? Nearly all of our 'bottom' class finished up with nine or ten 'School Certificates (GCSE now). Whereas nearly all those in the 'Alpha' and 'Beta' classes only had one or two, with distinction in each. The reason for this is simple. Our teachers didn't think we had much chance, and so put us in for everything, while the top classes specialised in one or two subjects only, and only took those exams. Now, forty or fifty years have passed, and it looks like all us 'nitwits' really were the brains of our year!

Sheila

My earliest memories of going to the pictures (never the cinema) was to be taken by my parents, usually on a Friday evening (pay day) to see light hearted films, comedies and musicals, by artists like Shirley Temple, Deanna Durbin, Fred Astaire, George Fornby and Old Mother Riley, to name but a few. This would always be at the Rock Cinema, at the bottom of Alum Rock Road, close to Saltley Gas Works. I can remember the magic of seeing colour – Walt Disney's animated film of Snow White and the Seven Dwarves – A classic to this day.

Sheila (far right) with group.

Not long after my fifth birthday, when my mother and her eldest sister, Aunt Eva, took myself and some of my cousins – about seven of us in all – to a matinee at the West End Cinema in town to see Robin Hood with Errol Flynn. We waited for the 33 tram to take us from the top of Holloway Head. We were all very excited by the prospect of this wonderful day out. Mom and Aunt Eva were counting out the change to pay for the tram fare and we were a few coppers short.

"Don't forget", my Aunt said to me, "if the conductor asks you, you're not five yet!"

We boarded the tram and every time the conductor passed a little voice could be heard repeating, "I'm not five yet, I'm not yet five!" amid a lot of shushing from the others.

We arrived at the West End in plenty of time, and we were ushered, by our elders, down to the front row. We thought we had been treated to the best seats in the cinema, and we sat with our heads right back and our eyes wide open, spellbound! A nudge came from the right, with the message, 'pass it on', provided each of us with a doorstep of crusty bread and butter followed by lumps of black pudding and, believe it or not, a jar of pickled onions. All of this was coming from an attaché case my aunt had open at her feet. Is it any wonder this memory has remained with me so vividly for over sixty years!

I don't remember going to the pictures much during the War years, not until I returned home from being evacuated. We had been bombed out in 1940 and had to leave Saltley. My parents had bought a little newsagents and tobacconists shop in

Ledsam Street, Ladywood. This really started out as back-to-back houses that had been knocked through to turn the house at the front into the shop, while the one at the back was the living quarters.

There were four cinemas in walking distance from the shop. 'The Edgbaston', on Monument Road, with a large foyer upstairs, red carpet, Lloyd Loom furniture and a statue. It was very swish. There was 'The Crown', on Icknield Port Road, a very good second choice, then there was 'The Lyric' at the Sandpitts, and 'The Regent', in Ledsam Street, otherwise known as 'The Ledsam', or by it's much more popular name, 'The Louse', for obvious reasons! This was only about one hundred yards from the shop.

The programmes were changed three times a week at all the cinemas, and there was a completely new programme just for Sunday. All of these were double features so in one week there was a possible twenty-four films to see, if you were so inclined. The films were continuous from about 1 pm until 10 pm. You would have come in from the light outside into nearly complete darkness. An usherette would show you to a seat with a torch. you with your eyes fixed on the big screen. You usually came in half way through a film, so you would watch the latter half, picking up the story as best you could. Then would come a newsreel and perhaps, if you were lucky, a short cartoon or travel film, followed by the second feature film, and 'trailers' showing flashes of forthcoming attractions.

Usually there would be an interval here, when the lights were raised, and ice cream would be on sale at the front of the theatre by the same usherettes who show you to your seats. It always seemed to be Midland Counties Ice Cream. I think they may have been the only manufacturers at this time, but they completely disappeared during, and for a long time after, the war. It would be now that the main film would begin – the one that was showing when you came in. When you recognised what was happening, and you were able to piece together the two halves, you would leave, sometimes reluctantly! "This is where I came in" originates from these occasions.

Of the four cinemas mentioned, I remember the old 'Louse' with much affection. It was run by staff of 'mature' years, with a Margaret Rutherford look-a-like in the ticket box where you paid 7d (3p) to sit in the front, 10d (4p) to sit in the middle, and a shilling (5p) to sit at the back. There was no balcony, just stalls that sloped towards the screen, and no-one would be surprised of one of the many cats that seemed to roam around jumped on your lap and made itself comfy.

Standing on the wide steps outside was the doorman. He was very proud of the uniform he wore, even though it must have been at least ten sizes too big. The coat was touching the floor, and he was constantly looking up his sleeves for his nearly white gloves that hung on his hands. We reckoned that he must have had at least a couple of copies of 'News of the World' stuffed in the lining of his hat in order that he could see and hear!

Saturday afternoon matinees at the Louse saw large queues of kids waiting to pay their 3d (1p) to see Buster Crabbe as Flash Gordon, Johnny Weisemuller as Tarzan, or Bill Boyd as Hopalong Cassidy, backed up by a couple of cartoons. Then at three the stampede was on, as all the kids burst out and filled the street in one mass, some hitting their thighs and riding imaginary horses, pointing a finger and shouting 'BANG! You're dead". Others twanged imaginary bows and arrows, some whooping and howling, and at the same time patting their hands on their mouths with their hands. We always knew what film had been showing that afternoon by their actions, ranging from beating their chests, accompanied by Tarzan yells, cowboys and Indians (as above), to sword and fist fights. This mayhem would be the signal for my Dad to position himself on the shop doorstep, legs astride and hands behind his back, to stop the invasion of the 'howmuchers', as he called them, all of them wanting to know the prices of the small range of toys that would be on display in the bay window that backed onto the pavement. Any little luxuries like these would, of course, be in short supply in the 1940s.

Yes, going to the pictures filled a lot of our lives, and was the main enjoyment of both the young and the older generation. It's a bit different today when a family of four has to spend a small fortune on an evening out, not to mention a car to get there.

If something like we enjoyed as teenagers was available to youth today, perhaps we wouldn't see so many groups of them, with no-where to go and nothing to do. The devil makes work for idle hands! So how about bringing back all the so-called fleapits of yester year. Wouldn't it be great?

The Children always enjoy hearing everyone's life stories.

Stan & Joyce

Were you alive in the war?

Bridget, Tanya, Joyce, Laura and Stan.

Stan: Yes. Well, I was at work when it first started. Then I had to go in the army, and that was it, really, I did much the same as anybody else. There was all sorts of bombing going on, and yes, I suppose it was scary, like the war that's going on now, you know. Yes, it was scary when the sirens went and you had to run down into the air raid shelters. When you're young, (we were in our teens), I'd left school, you're less scared.

I went to Yardley Wood School, in School Road, just below the church. Where Yardley Wood Church is, that used to be a little infant school, the juniors and the seniors were further down School Road, and I went there, all through my school days.

Joyce: And I went to Colmore Road School.

Did you ever get the cane?

Stan: Yes, I was talking in the lines, you know, when they blew the whistle or rung the bell, you'd got to line up and march into your class. I was at the back, talking to my pal when I should have been marching in the lines.

There were two of us or three of us, and this science master, he used to have a cane, and you got three on either hand. You had to hold out your hands, and you got three strokes on either one with the cane. Oh, it made your hands tingle! But you didn't talk again. It didn't bother us, you know, just having the cane didn't bother us that much. It was the only time I ever had it.

Do you have any friends from school?

Stan: Oh yes, I've got friends I've known all my life, one, we went to school together, and we used to live a few doors away from each other, not far from here, in Ida Road, off School Road.

Did you use different objects in the past?

Stan: You mean like ink pens? Oh yes. The pens were pen nibs,

Stan and Joyce enjoy a cuppa with a friend.

and we had inkwells, on the desk with red ink and blue ink. You had to wipe the pens if you wanted to change colour, it was like a loose nib you used to have stuck in the end of the pen, and the inkwells, someone used to fill the inkwells every Monday morning. No Biros then! Yes, we used to drop the ink…

Joyce: There were always splashes on the table!

Stan sharing a joke.

Did you play games?

Stan: We used to wind a piece of string round a stick, stick it into the ground, and spin the top from it. March, it used to come round. We used to play games with sticks, and newspaper, and make kites. March was always windy, so we made kites in March. Hopscotch. You have that now, don't you? And then there was Jackstones, where you threw them into the air and had to catch them. Then marbles used to come round, you'd suddenly see somebody with a bag of marbles, and then everybody would get their marbles out, and if you hit the marble, it was yours.

And cigarette cards! You'd have these picture cards in the cigarette packets, they used to come in sets of fifty and you'd try to collect the set, cricketers, or film stars, and everybody smoked then. You'd say " You got forty-five, I'll swap you for twenty- two" until you got the set. Then we used to skewer them in a line against the fence, and try to knock them down. These were games that didn't cost a lot of money.

There were what you'd call, "coppers on the beat", and at every lamp post there was a bench, and you could only cross the road there, and if you crossed at the wrong place the kid that was "on" would chase all the others across the road. Remember, there were no cars on the roads, you just wouldn't see them. Any one who came along in a car was rich. There were horses and carts, bringing the milk and the bread, and the coal. You couldn't play in the road, these days.

Skipping! We'd have a skipping rope across the road and there would be fifteen, twenty kids all skipping, and if you tripped up, you'd be turning the rope. All these games used

Stan showing the children his valuable medal collection.

to come round the same time every year. That was our entertainment. We were never bored. In those days we could light a little fire in our back garden, get a potato out of our mum's vegetable basket, and try and roast it on the fire in the garden. Oh, they were hard, but we still ate the things, don't know how we survived! Or we'd cook a stew in a tin. You'd try and cook any thing on the fire. All those sort of things, obviously, you can't do it these days. The things we used to do, they'd say you mustn't do that because it's dangerous.

Of course, roller skates used to come round the same time every year, and hopscotch, and marbles, and we'd collect blackberries in a big basin, and there was knocking the knockers on people's doors and running!

What kind of books did you read?

Stan: I don't remember reading many books, although we did used to go to the library. We always had comics. I used to always have a comic book a week, which was about tuppence, a Wizard, or a Beano. A wet day, we'd go to our pal's with a pile of comics, and if I didn't have some of his, I'd have some off him and he'd have one or two of mine, but I don't really remember many books, to be honest.

Joyce: I used to love reading.

In the past were there magazines?

Stan: Yes, there were always girls' books and magazines, yes. There were books for boys, and books for girls, like now.

Did you have bicycles?

Stan: We had bicycles, but they were for richer people. The first bike I ever had of my own was when I started work. And it cost five pounds. That was new. I got it from the Stratford Road. My first job was at a warehouse in the Bullring, the old Bullring, of course, but the place was bombed, so I had to find another job.

Joyce: I worked at Cadbury's, the chocolate factory. I never go in the chocolate shop. Once a year we have a party from Cadbury's, but I never buy chocolate.

Did you have any hobbies?

Stan: We had little crystal sets, little radios, we used to make them ourselves.
We didn't go on many trips. We went to Lickey Hills, that was a good day out. We went to the Science Museum. And they took us on a walk round Trittiford Park, to look at the plants.
   Before the bus garage was built, they used to hold a fair there, once a year, and there was one held in Kings Norton. It used to be on the knob of the hill, because I remember walking up to it. I can't remember what time of the year it came, but it used to come every year. The only time I ever went away was with the boy scouts, two weeks on camp, that was somewhere in Staffordshire. I was in St Albans

Scouts, in Conybere Street. It was strange to go to scouts that far away, but the pals I'd known all my life lived out that way and they used to go to that church. The one pal got us all to join with him in the same scouts. You'd go on company marches every Sunday morning after church. We had a week in Colwyn Bay in 1937 with my family. It was the first holiday I ever remember, then after that, the war had started, but we went to Blackpool for a week.

What were your favourite things at school?

Stan: Well, I was never very good at gym and sport. I used to run in the school sports, the same as everybody else, you know, the egg and spoon race, and the sack race, same as everybody else, but I was never any good. I was always last. I love to watch gymnastics on the television. We played a bit of football, but I was never any good. Cricket, I couldn't play cricket, I was always out first time!

Stan, Joyce and friends sharing good times over a cup of tea.

5. OTHER STORIES

Birmingham Lives 2001

This was a project which ran in 2001, and directly led to the AGElink project. *Birmingham Lives 2001* recorded the stories of residents, many of which took part in the AGElink project. In this, the first project, and indeed the spark which created Birmingham Lives, Community Art workers (Ann Heath, Chris Callow, Marcus Belben and Nicola Thorpe) used tape machines to record participants speaking, and edit those conversations with the participants.

Birmingham Lives 2001 aimed to interview a number of older people from a variety of backgrounds, living in sheltered housing, residential and nursing care in Birmingham. In this book only stories from residents of Brookmeadow Court are published. All the participants took the opportunity to write about what they wanted, not only in terms of content, but also in their own style. Some are considerably longer than others; some cover a whole life, while others cover only a small part; some used art to illustrate; one used a short piece of fiction. Both the stories and the means by which they are recorded are unique.

Marcus Belben - Birmingham Lives

Marcus with Kitty, then aged 104.

74

Barbara

I grew up in Aberdeen and first came to Birmingham during the Second World War. We were conscripted down here on war work, me and twelve other girls who were from Glasgow. They told us on the Tuesday to be ready and we moved on Friday, only three days' notice to pack everything up and go. We met on the train going down to New Street station, which was a real dump even then, and taken in a wee pick-up van to our different lodging houses. We had no say in where we wanted to go, you were simply

Barbara and Jock.

told that that was your billet. We were paying 5 shillings a week, and the government paid another pound towards our board and lodging.

I had to lodge in Painswick Road, Hall Green with another girl called Mary. The landlady was a very nice woman, but very particular. When we first got there, she asked us to take our shoes off. Mary said, "My feet are not dirty!" "No," she replied, "but my carpets are clean!" So we took them off. Then she took us into her front room and explained that that was where we would be eating. Except that we never got any meals. That same afternoon, after we had checked in at Birmingham Small Arms in Small Heath, we were sitting twiddling our thumbs for ages, expecting to get our tea. Finally I asked the woman if we could have some food, but she simply replied "You know that food's on ration, don't you? You can't have it. You can get your breakfast tomorrow morning!" By that time, it was only about 4:00 in the afternoon. When we went to bed she told us not to make a noise and showed us up to the bedroom. There was only one double bed between us. Mary asked, "Where's the other bed?" The woman just pointed and said "That's it. You're only paying five shillings a week!" So on our first night we went off to bed without even a cup of tea or cocoa.

For breakfast the next morning we had some bread and a wee scraping of margarine that was no bigger than a 20p. The landlady told us "Don't go over the score now, that's your ration." You should have heard what we said about her when she went out of the room! She had made us some sandwiches for our dinner, but Mary looked in them when we got to the BSA and said "That's cows udder!". I didn't know what a cow's udder was so she told me. She'd eaten it at home in Scotland as well because the meat rations never went far enough. So when it came to dinner time we all got our sandwiches out together and when the others found out what we were eating, the things they said to us! Everyone was in the same boat, though, they all had black pudding or something else cheap. The whole area was very poverty-stricken.

That first day, we were shown around the BSA and given our jobs to do. I had never seen a machine in my life before! I used to be a domestic servant in Edinburgh in some very posh houses - I wasn't working class until I came down here! I was put on the machines to make the breach blocks of a Sten Gun, but I was useless at the work. I was on a milling machine first and I broke so many pieces of it that they moved me onto a drilling machine but I never got very far with that either. I always worked very hard, but instead of moving the drill down slowly I would bang it down and more often than not break the drill bit. The fitter, Horace, who was in charge, got fed up of me really quickly!

We used to have to go in at seven in the morning and we came out about 5 at night. You had to show your identity card as you went in through the tiny wee trapdoor at the front. It's a good job I wasn't as fat as I am now, I'd have never got in! Our wages were very poor. Anyone who says we used to get a big wage during the war is wrong. Ours was only about three pounds a week, and the men didn't get much either.

We were always told that we were lucky to be paid at all. That annoyed me. I used to say "I never asked to come down here, you know. I'm only doing this for my country's sake." Except that wasn't really true! I was only doing it because they told me to! We were fed up with the conditions after only a week, and I was really homesick for Scotland, so Mary and I decided to go home again. But when we got to Edinburgh, the police were waiting for us at the other end. We were turned around and sent straight back on the train. In the war, you had to do what you were told.

Eventually, I got really fed up with the factory so I asked for a transfer to the BSA on Waverley Road. I used to make wheels for folding bicycles that parachutists used. I was taught how to lace the wheels but I was no better at that, than at drilling! I would hate to see a parachutist get on one of my bikes. I don't think I would dare to watch. I stayed there for about six months, until I got fed up with it and decided to move on again. My landlady suggested that I should try for a job on the buses, but I had to have three references to be accepted! They probably thought I was a spy because I had moved around so much! It took the references ages to come through because they had to send up to Scotland for them, but eventually they arrived and I got the job. That's when my life in Birmingham really started.

For the first three weeks, I was on the job with another person who showed me what to do. I had to learn all the different numbers for punching the tickets so I could tell if someone was fiddling their fare. When I had passed out of training,

I was put on the Number 8 bus on the inner circle route.

It was a busy route, especially where the bus crossed over Stoney Lane near the Stratford Road. There was normally a large crowd waiting there to go up to the BSA and often the bus would be full, so you would have to put a chain across the door to stop anyone else climbing on. I was quite nervous about that, and asked what I should do if someone jumps on under the chain. My supervisor said "Just give them a crack on the head with your ticket wrack". I believed her, because the wrack was long enough, but the first time I did it was the last! We were crossing the Stratford Road when a man came rushing up and tried to jump on. As soon as he put his head through the chain I yelled "Full up!" and cracked him hard on the head. What a sound! And he just disappeared! Fell down and I couldn't see him anywhere. The bus drove off and carried on

Barbara in her bus uniform.

round the route so it took a full hour to come back to that spot again and all that time, I was worried sick - I thought I might have killed him! When we got back to the spot, I half expected to see him still lying in the road, but I couldn't even see any blood on the floor. No-one ever complained about me or mentioned it again, but I got the fright of my life!

Some of the driving was dangerous enough. We used to go round one traffic island by Small Heath Park with the bus going so fast it was nearly on 2 wheels! One time my friend, Eva Gordon, was standing at the back of the bus talking to me and leaning up against the pole in the middle of the door when we went round the roundabout, and before you knew it, she'd fallen out! She was fine, though. I saw her running after the bus to get back on!

I was a terrible conductress. Every three months, good timekeepers would be paid an extra twenty-five shillings, but I never got them! It was a shame that I never made the grade, but it didn't really bother me. I've got a thick skin and a tongue in my head, so I was never normally reported, even though I would forget to ring the bell because I was chatting to passengers. There would always be a line of buses behind mine because we were taking so long! Before one evening shift, I was pulled up by one of the inspectors who said "You're late again, Scotty". I just told him to get stuffed! Of course, he reported me and I had to write an explanation for the head inspector about what I had said. All I put was "At ten minutes past four, I told him to get stuffed!" I didn't even get into trouble for that - I was simply told to try not to do it again!

I wasn't afraid of talking back to the passengers - sometimes you had to! Dogs always had to go up the stairs, though people would try to sneak the little ones in. You'd be collecting their fares and suddenly their coats would start barking at you! One day, as we went along Stratford Road with a very crowded bus, a man got on with a dog and went straight for a seat downstairs. When I told him to go upstairs he takes one look at me and says "Stick it up yer arse!" So I said "Well, if you can do the same with your dog you can come inside!" What he called me was nobody's business!

I always remember when things went wrong as well. There was a chip shop at Aston Cross where there would usually be quite a crowd waiting to get on. We were often there for some time, so I would pop out and buy me and the driver some chips. A couple of times I'd come out of the shop to find there was no bus waiting! The passengers used to help you out during the war, so when they thought the last one was on the bus, they'd press the bell and the bus would go off. Without me! I had to wait until another one appeared to get a lift to catch my bus up. Half the time, I didn't catch it until Nechells Green, and the chips were cold by then!

Another day, none of the bells were working so I had to use my whistle instead. But the first time I blew it, my false teeth flew right out of my mouth and up the bus! It took me ages to find them, with all the passengers looking at me, wondering why I was crawling around the floor. After that, I didn't blow my whistle any more so the driver never knew when to drive off. We were so late getting back to the depot at Saltley that I was reported to the inspector. All he did was laugh and told me to get my teeth seen to.

I don't think we ever ran anyone over, but I was threatened a lot by the passengers, especially when the pubs threw out, and at the end of shifts at the Lucas factory. They used to come barging out of there like a lot of animals. When that happened, you had to stand sideways in the doorway to direct people into the bus - left hand pointing them to the top deck, right hand pointing them inside. One day, I was titivating myself up, putting a bit of lipstick on in the mirror half way up the stairs, when we got to Lucas just as the hooter went. This crowd of men came running out and barged their way onto the bus before I could get downstairs, and took me with them. I landed right at the top of the bloody stairs! And I couldn't get back down again to do my job! Just my luck that an inspector turned up and I could hear him shouting for me "Where are you this time, Scotty?" I said "I'm up here". "Well the passengers are down here!!" he yelled. "Scotty, you'll never improve will you!"

I was a terrible conductress! I took a lot of money though. I was the fool who'd go and collect all the fares and then I'd have to sit and count all the money at the end of the day. If you were sensible, you wouldn't take too much! We used to go down Belgrave Road which we called the "Burma Road" because that was where the men in turbans would get on. They were very nice, and when they gave me their fares I'd get a little bottles of scent as well! Ever so kind!

I loved working on the buses. We had a really good life. There used to be dances held in the garage, and you could get a cup of tea and a piece of cake after your shift, which is more than you got at your digs. And I met my husband, Jock, on the buses. He came out of the army in 1946 but couldn't find good work in Scotland so he came down to Birmingham and joined the buses.

I first saw him at the Highgate Road depot. We were having our cup of tea when he walked in, and I thought straight away "Oh he's a nice fellow, there, I'm having him." So I went over and bought him a cup of tea - big hearted of me, it only cost a penny! I had to catch him quick because my pals, Big Kath and Jean, were interested in him as well, so we were always waiting for him to come in, buying him tea and fussing over him. He started off as a conductor, but then he learnt to drive and I became his conductress. The first time he was going to take me out, he had booked tickets for the Hippodrome and arranged everything, when I was put on the late shift at the last minute so I couldn't go. That was the way it went - every time he booked something I was late!

We got married in 1948 and stayed down in Birmingham for twelve months. Jock was longing to get back to Scotland, though, so we sold up everything we had and went back. Jock got a transfer so he stayed on the buses but I couldn't get one. I was a good woman, but not a good conductress! It was a sad day for me when I left.

Scotland wasn't the same anymore. Everything had changed and there wasn't the work. You have to go where your bread and butter is, so we only stayed there for six months and then settled back here. We've been in Birmingham over fifty years now.

Doris

I didn't know he'd put our names down for this place. Suddenly Pete said to me, "Haven't you got your name down for this place?"

I said, "I don't know". So he wrote, and next thing it came through, there was a flat at Brook Meadow Court, and I took it. I'm comfortable. I've got a lounge, a kitchen, a bathroom, what else do I want? We're all about the same age, over seventy-five and I get on with most people. Well, there's no one I don't get on with. I miss the garden. It wasn't too big but it was enough. I enjoyed my garden. We both did. We'd spend days on the garden, but after he'd gone it was too much for me, so fair enough. Then this came along and I took it. I don't regret it one bit. I've been here nine years now. It's a long time, isn't it?

Within a week of getting in here, I left my house for my son to deal with. He rang me up and said, "I've sold it, but I've refused the offer".

I said, "Oh my God, what have you gone and done that for".

He said, "They were trying to knock it down too much. Leave it with me". He rang me up two weeks later and said it was gone. The same people had come back and improved the offer. You could hang on to it for twelve months, but you've still got to pay the rates, haven't you. It's a big decision you have to make when you break your home up.

I've lived all my life in Birmingham. We were bombed out at the start of the war, in Christmas 1940. We were married in January 1940, and Bernard was called up in the July. By the next Christmas he had gone straight into the siege of Tobrok, North Africa. I had a map on the wall and when he moved I pin pricked it on the map.

If you got a letter it was a least two months old to begin, and then after a couple of years they got the airmails in and it wasn't so bad. I didn't see him for four years and then I get this one letter just before the Christmas: "I really truly am coming home". He had five weeks leave and then he was out in the August, so he actually did five years in all. He came out with sixty-four quid. That was just what they gave you after you'd done so many years. It was a pittance really. I think I got a pound a week Army money.

I'd worked; I'd got to go to work. I was bombed out and then I got another house, so I had a home for him to go to, which was something. He hadn't changed one bit.

When Pete, my son, was about three or four and Sue was about six or seven, it was eight or nine years after the war and he had a letter come out of the blue, he'd got to do a fortnight in the Army. So he went, and he was the only one, as far as we know, out of his Battalion. He was a printer's compositor you see, and his firm was very good, they understood. It annoyed me at the time, he was a tradesman. He was twenty-eight when he was called up. There were some around me that had never worked all their lives, they were scroungers, and they were straight to the British Small Arms in Small Heath and got a job, and never went to the Army at all. They should have got the scroungers in first.

I remember once this lad lived not far away, lost his fingers and got scarred all down his face in the war, I met him on the bus. When we got off I started walking back together, as he only lived down the street from us. Someone shouted out, "Are you home again?" The insolence, and from someone who hadn't lifted a finger. But still, you get over it.

He was in the siege of Tobrok for ten months, and then he went into Italy, into the Italian campaign. He came home with about six medals, but what good are them? But still. He was one of the anti-aircraft guns. Before he went to Perry Barr Park, and everyone said, "Aren't you lucky!"

They moved out of there in October, November, and down to London before embarkation. They fetched one plane down in Perry Barr Park. They were only there for three weeks. I think they were a bit too good.

The people with him were a Birmingham crowd, who were in the reserves. They were youngsters, eighteen, nineteen, twenty. They'd joined up for a bit of fun before the war, didn't think anything would come of it. Of course they got called in.
I was able to send him parcels. I heard afterwards, they used to go around saying, "Hey, Smith's got a parcel!"

Apparently they used to share it out. I worked in the Market Hall and my friends there used to say, "When you sending a parcel, Doll?" One would bring cigarettes and another something else. I sent magazines and detective stories, anything for them to do, because they were bored. At first they were busy, but after a while they were moved to Italy and then they stopped in Italy. I think they stopped in Tripoli.

He got his old job back. While he was away they'd got the relatives in. Well, he was a printer's compositor. You don't do a job like that unless you know what you are doing. He worked on the Birmingham Mail for quite some time. They have to make the blocks to print off. Each letter is tiny, and it's a skilled job.

My first home was in Balsall Heath. At the back of where I lived there was a terrace, and this bomb came down and the hole where it went. It was a huge crater. My father said, "I've never seen anything like it". There were twelve houses in that terrace, and luckily not one person was hurt. They were all in shelters. But it cracked all the walls in my house. I'd gone to my Mum's to sleep, so I wasn't there that night. Funnily enough a couple of weeks before I'd had Mum and Dad up to my place to sleep there. It was much healthier than where they were in Small Heath.

Anyway, the walls were all cracked and there was a notice up to say I wasn't to go upstairs. My Dad helped me and got all the furniture downstairs, and I moved out. My sister had got a house with a spare room, so I packed most of my furniture in there, took my piano to Mum's to look after it. After about six months I got a house. The old dear died and I went for it, to have a house for my husband to come back to, and that was in Small Heath.

We didn't have a shelter when it started. We used to stand on the cellar steps, me and my sister. You'd be up all night to six o'clock in the morning when the all clear would go. You'd get washed, have something to eat, and then you'd be at work at seven. I used to be at the market, three mornings at seven.

I was a cashier and bookkeeper at the market. When I was twelve, thirteen and fourteen I passed the Grammar school, three times, couldn't go. I cried my eyes out the first time. I thought it was marvellous to sit in that hall and do that exam. I sat three times, because it was an honour for the school. I didn't mind. I was the eldest of five and couldn't afford it. My Dad had got an Aunt who had got a chain of pawnbroking shops. So, of all things, they decided to put me in the pawnbroking. I hated, I loathed it. At nineteen I was managing a shop for twenty-four bob a week, and I'd got a fourteen-year-old girl working for me. I saw this advert in the Mail. I didn't say anything to my Mum and Dad, and I wrote after it. To my surprise I had an answer.

The job was in the market. When I applied the bloke, my boss said, "Why do you want to leave?"

I said, "Well, I've got as far as I've got, as far as I'll go. I can't go any higher and I don't like it".

I got the job. I started on twenty-five bob a week and I finished up on just over three pound a week and bonus. Printing at that time was highly paid and he was getting just over three pounds a week, so for six months we did very well, until he was called up.

I got Monday morning off one week, Monday afternoon off the next week, and all Monday the week after. You finished at one o'clock on Saturday. You see I was working nine 'til nine the last job on Saturday. Those were the days, you see. It was marvellous when you finished five or six, and to have a Saturday off I could go dancing with my husband. We used to go out locally, and we used to go to Tony's in Town. Any special dances we went there. There was Moseley and Balsall Heath Institute. That was where I met my husband.

I'd never recognise the market, now. I'd come at that bus, up Digbeth, jump off just past the church and into the side entrance of the Market Hall. I enjoyed working in town. We worked hard, but we were paid well. It was a high-class fish and poultry. We used to do a roaring trade. We got five cashiers, and I was over them. There were ten men as well.

I remember when the Market Hall was bombed by the IRA. When I got there in the morning, you can't imagine it. You had to pick your way through the water pipes in the Bullring, where they'd been fighting the fires all night. There were no windows in the Market Hall, and the roof got bombed off. The scales – you didn't have automatic ones – my boss wouldn't have them. All the weights were frozen solid to the table. Without a top to the Market Hall it could get cold in the winter.

When the War was on we had ration books. Everyone was entitled to so much. There was bacon, butter (you very rarely saw butter), margarine, cheese, meat, bread, and at one point there were potatoes too. Eventually it eased. Of course, being on the market, I was able to get fish, occasional rabbit or chicken. We were able to live reasonably well. For people who just had the rations, I don't know how they did it.

We didn't have as much fish as we had before the war. We sold out every day. The fish mostly came in from Grimsby, the plaice and cod. We had Lemon Soles, Dover Soles and Salmon direct from Aberdeen.

We were one of thousands effected by the war. I hope, to God, it never happens again for all you young people.

Flos

My Dad was a Cockney; he used to talk proper cockney. He was in the Army when he was fourteen, boy service, and he went to Salisbury. He met my mother, and she was only about sixteen when she married him. They went straight to India with the Army. She had two children there, brought them back with her. She had a marvellous life in India. They were treated like ladies.

That wasn't me, it was my brother and sister. One brother would be a hundred now, and I've got the daughter of the eldest sister, my niece, visiting tomorrow, and she's seventy-five. I'm one of the youngest. My eldest sister used to talk ever so nice. Nothing like us, because she was taught like that, out there, in the schools. They had a good life out there, with servants looking after them. They were out there fifteen years, and they came back to Portsmouth, and they started having more children.

He finished his time, after twenty-five years. When he finished in the Army, my mother had a sister in Birmingham. She said, if you come here you'd get a job in Birmingham. They came and settled in Birmingham, got a house, and he couldn't get a job. He was even out of work when I was a little kid. There was no work about, see. He used to go and get up in the night, sticking posters on the walls, anything to earn a shilling. It was a terrible life in those days I remember even though I was a little kid.

He used to get a pension from the army, I think, five pounds a quarter. We used to wait for him to get that pension and he'd throw us half a crown each. He was a marvellous man. Brought the kids up to know right from wrong.

Then they went to Dunlops, where they used to do the rubber. They used to come home covered in rubber, all in the hair, the shirt, everywhere. He stopped in Dunlop for years and years. He died when he was sixty-three. He was a fine man, my father; a proper Army man. You daren't do anything without asking him. You had to do what he said. Things were different then. Today, they don't listen to their mother or their father. And I can't understand why they leave home. Our Julie she's twenty-three, nearly twenty-four, she's gone and bought herself a house! "Stop at home and once you get married!"

"No", she said, "we'll leave home now." They've got a lovely house up Kingstanding. Can't understand it, really. Still, it's a different world today, isn't it?

In the end, my father ended up being a doorman at the picture house. Everyone knew him. He used to let all the kids in for nothing, round the back. There used to be picture houses everywhere then. He loved that job. He was working there when he died. My dad died in 1939, just as the war started. My mother never got over that. She wouldn't go to bed at the night, she wouldn't undress herself, you know, she never lived after that. I suppose some people don't.

Aston Hall used to be all Aston. They must have built these houses before the World War, and every one of these houses in Park Lane has got a tunnel to Aston Hall. In the Cellar there was a door built in and that led to Aston Hall. When my mother used to tell me I didn't believe it, but it was true. Just over the road from Aston Cross. We used to look at the clock to tell the proper time. It's been moved now. They've moved it up the road. There used to be a great big Ansell's brewery. That's gone now. It's all one big garage.

I lived with my mum until I got married. Then I moved up the other end of Aston. When I go and see it now I can't believe it. They've built that motorway right through Aston, right along Lichfield Road, and all the houses had to come down, to build that motorway. We had a nice little house; it was a little cottage house. I went to live up the other way in Aston, towards Six Ways.

I didn't move from Aston until 1960, to new blocks of flats. My husband, Harry, used to say, "Come and live in the country, in Erdington! It's got all grass and that." He loved it there. But he came from Summer Lane. It wasn't a rough part, really, but it is now. Very kind people down there. All poor people, who helped one another. He was a

Flos's parents.

proper Summer Laney, my husband. He used to say, "Hello our wench!"

I haven't been there for years. Newtown Road, with the markets and that - the house that Jack built. You ever heard of that? I used to do all our shopping in the house that Jack built. I think it got bombed in the war. A lot of it round there got bombed down. We used to get ready for bed and the sirens would go. Run down the shelter, you couldn't go to bed, you had to stop all night.

Trams by the Aston Cross.

Moved in to my husband's mother's house in 1943. She said they were moving all of them out to Kingstanding, into new council houses. She said if you want this house you go and see the landlord, he'll let you have it, and he did. Five shilling a week, that was half a crown. So they were a good start for us. When he came out from the forces, I'd got a house there, and everything for him.

He was lucky really, because he was out of all the fighting. They had to look after Gibraltar, watch for the boats come in and all that. He had it easy. Stopped there all the time. And when he came back he got his old job back for ICI.

I worked all night, and sometimes we'd have to come in on Sunday as well, making bullets at ICI. I had started working there at fourteen, in 1936. But what our job was really, was making carburettors for AMAL Carburettors. Very well known, for all the motors. And, of course, all the men would go to the Isle of Man once a year, to watch the races. My husband was ever so interested. We had a motorbike before cars came out. He used to love his motorbike. We had a little Austin car, car number ASP. Isn't it funny how you can remember something like that?

I worked on a big capstan. You stand at the machine all day stringing the handle making screws. You daren't stop because if your numbers were down you didn't get paid. You stand there swinging the handle; there was no electricity, a great big belt taking it round. My husband was a piler. He used to pile all the metal down. We loved it there, we had lovely jobs.

I met him there. He took me to the pantomime, and it's been a pantomime ever since! He was a nice man. I couldn't get married straight away because our mother was still alive then, and I had to look after her. Other lads had joined the forces and she was still on her own on Park Lane. I stopped with her until she died in 1942 and I got married in 1943. The lads used to come home, my brothers, and I used to look after them. One got killed at Dunkirk. He was lovely. Another got shell shock. He was in the navy and they bombed the ship he was on, and when he got home he never got over it. He died. It was terrible, honestly, young chap being killed. Still that's war isn't it. We don't want to see another one.

After we got married he went to Gibraltar. When he came on leave after a while, we went to Blackpool for our honeymoon. After the war he came back and he had a skin complaint. I reckon it was the water or something. He had to keep having operations and operations. And his face was all scarred. That's what the war did to him. He had all his face skin grafted. But he was a happy bloke. He never worried. He looked after my brother's kids.

We had street celebrations. My brother saved all his Joeys, thre'penny pieces, what we would call five pence now. He saved them and saved them, and when he came out of the forces he threw them to the kids in the street. All the kids were fighting for them. It was just after, they went out of currency.

There was a farthing, ha'penny, and a penny. There were four farthings in a penny. Then it went to thre'penny, three pence, then a shilling, twelve pennies, then two shilling, then half a crown, two shilling and six, then five shilling, then ten shilling which is a modern fifty pence piece, but they were mostly notes. When I started working I had ten shilling a week. I used to give eight shilling to my mother then two for myself. We used to go to the pictures, and everything, all week. We'd never seen a pound, which was twelve shillings. It was all notes then, and if you had a pound you'd be rich. When I married my husband he was earning thirty-seven shillings a week, which is not a lot. You had to be very careful.

I used to walk to work straight up the Aston road to Whitton. Could have got the tram but it wasn't worth waiting for. They used to have a fair, the Onion Fair in Whitton. When that was on you couldn't get on the trams or anything. One night we were standing by the bottom, and they were all running and our mum said, "What are you all running for?" The lion had got loose, and there was the lion running down from the fair to the Aston Cross. When they caught him, he dropped down dead, the lion did, from shock I think. That fair was well known across the country. Always used to queue up to go in there.

Flos (second from left) with work colleagues, 1945.

There were a lot of trams. The one I used to like was the one to the Lickey Hills. The tram used to go right up and it was quite a ride out. I did my courting on the Lickey Hills. From the Cross you could get one to Whitton, to Bromford, Town, so it was good. Used to love the trams. When you went to the Lickeys there was a piece up at the top, to look out over Birmingham. We used to love the Lickey Hills, and the Malvern Hills, too.

We had a caravan. Everyone used to have a holiday in our caravan in Evesham. It was lovely, right on the river. He used to love fishing. Friday night, straight from work, straight down to the caravan. We used to stop there until Sunday night. We loved that.

My husband gets a marvellous pension from ICI. I never had one because they said if you both have one you're paying it all out on tax, and I still get it. For me it goes up every year, so you can't grumble about that can you? It means you can live in comfort. Mind you, if you've got the money you have to pay more rent. If you don't you don't have to.

In the end my husband had Alzheimer's. They don't know they have anything wrong with them, but the person who has to look after them has a terrible life. He used to get up in the night and I'd say, "Where are you going?"

And he'd say, "I've got to get up for work, I don't want to lose my job." He'd been retired twenty years. You couldn't tell him. He'd get dressed, to get the bus, and I used to follow him and bring him back. Terrible that.

Looked after him for three years, and in the end, pneumonia. Still, if it's your husband you've got to look after them. That's what we were taught, anyhow. It was in Erdington, and, of course, being in a high rise block of flats, I could never find him. He used to have a bet every day. That was his hobby. He used to creep out and I used to have to go and find him. We used to have some laughs, though. Wild Green, Chester Road. That's where we lived. He started wondering off in the night, and the council said, "We found your bloke in the garden". He never knew where he was. He hated it.

Six months after he died I had this stroke. I was just getting over it. You never know what is going to happen. That's Life.

Everything is all so different now. When I came here (Brookmeadow Court) I didn't know where I lived. I don't now really. I haven't been able to go out since I've moved here. They've taken me out in the wheel chair to some things. I'm getting to know, because the man who takes me to the club takes me all different ways round.

When I had this stroke I was twelve stone and I went down to six stone. Nobody knew me! I was always dieting, couldn't get my weight off, then I go down to six stone. One thing about me is I'm in no pain. I mean in here they've all got bad legs and that. This leg's dead, and I don't know where it is when I'm walking, but it doesn't hurt. Nor this arm. It's a nuisance, but it never hurts me. I couldn't swallow and I couldn't talk for two months when I had my stroke, and that's terrible. You're trying to talk and you think you're talking but nothing is coming out. Sometimes now it goes, but it comes back again.

It's worse for a man. There's a man in the Stroke club in a wheel chair, only about fifty-five and he can't walk or talk. I feel so sorry for him. He can laugh, we have a good laugh, but he can't answer you when you talk to him. You've got to be thankful if you've got you're health.

When seventy-one year-old widow, Flo Knight suffered a severe stroke she was told that she would never walk again. She talks to Andrew Hillier.

"I can remember sitting on the settee, reading the paper and drinking a cup of tea, when all of a sudden I felt strange. 'What's happening to me' I thought, 'I can't feel a thing'.

Everything went numb and I started to fall towards the floor. As I fell I tried to speak but couldn't open my mouth. The next thing I knew I was on the floor, unable to move, staring straight at the carpet. I didn't know what was going on. My whole body just didn't feel like it was there anymore. Luckily my friend, Joan, was in the room and rushed to the phone to call an ambulance. By the time it arrived I had totally blacked out.

The next day I woke up and didn't know what had happened. I tried to move both my right leg and arm but nothing happened. When I tried to speak not even a sound came out. All I could remember was that I had been to Chester for the day and when I had came back I had fallen off the settee; everything afterwards was a blur.

When I saw the doctor he told me that I had suffered a severe stroke. He added that they were unsure about how much damage had been done, but they were certain that the chance of me making a fully recovery were slim. I was totally shocked. The previous year I had a minor stroke after my husband, Harry, had died, but I never imagined that anything like this could happen to me.

For two weeks I was unable to speak, and I could hardly move. All feeling had totally gone from down my right hand side, and I also found it difficult to eat and drink. In the space of two months my weight dropped from twelve to six stone, and I looked extremely frail. When my speech returned it was also severely slurred and people found it difficult to understand what I was saying. Suddenly over night I had become a little old lady.

All the time I had self-belief and kept thinking that I would recover. I was convinced it would only be a matter of time before I was back to my old self, and refused to believe that I would never be able to look after myself again.

I was particularly concerned about walking. I realised that if I was able to walk then at least I had some hope of being able to manage on my own. But, one day when I asked the doctor what my chances were, he simply said, 'Mrs Knight, you'll never walk again'. I simply refused to believe it. I ordered the nurse to bring me a walking stick and thought 'there is no way I'm going to accept it without a fight.

I remained in Selly Oak Hospital, Birmingham, for four months staring out of the same window and looking at the same tree blowing in the wind. All the time my family visited and I had constant physiotherapy and gradually, after time, I regained some strength in my right foot. I was told however, if I had not shown enough signs of recovery within six months, I would be sent to a nursing home. That was my worst nightmare, all my life I had been so independent and there was no way I was prepared to spend my last days in some home.

Then, one afternoon I was told that a place had been found for me at convalescent home for both mentally and physically disabled people. At the time there was no way I could have returned home, I still could not walk, my right arm was useless - I would never had managed to look after myself.

When I first arrived I thought they had placed me in some mental home. There were people who couldn't walk, and spoke through machines. There were also people with brain damage as well as people who had spent their whole lives in a wheel chair. Few had any chance of recovery, yet I still believed that I would be able to recover.

After the initial few days it really put into proportion how fortunate I had been in life. Many of these people had their whole lives ahead of them, I on the other hand was 71. I saw men in their twenties having to come to terms with spending the rest of the lives in a wheel chair - it inspired me to make the most of the mobility I had left.

After two months in the home I had managed to build enough strength in my right leg to allow me to walk short distances. And, just before Christmas I was told I would be allowed to return home. Finally, after six hard months I had achieved what I had set out to do - I had made it home.

Four years on, I have never fully recovered from the stroke. My right arm is totally useless and just hangs like a dead weight, and I only have limited mobility in my right leg. The stroke also affected my sense of smell, and taste. Sometimes when I eat my dinner I can't even taste what I've just eaten, and when people occasionally say, 'oh, what's that smell ?' I can never tell.

But you learn to cope. Each week I have a home help who does my washing, and cleans the flat. My family have also been brilliant, they constantly visit, and take me for days out in my wheel chair. I get frustrated occasionally, but you just have to pull yourself together and think positive thoughts. I just feel lucky because I'm still here."

Extract from YOURS, 16th May 1997, Andrew Hillier

George 'Jock'

I went into the army in February 1939 and did my training at Woolwich. When I passed out there we were sent to Brighton in the Royal Artillery but we only stayed for a couple of weeks when the War broke out. I think Hitler had been waiting for me to join up before he started anything! Very soon after the War had started they took my regiment over to France and we were based there near Lille. At first very little happened. The funny thing is that all the time we were in France and Belgium we never fired one round of ammunition for the very good reason that we didn't have any. It was just a farce. If we had to fight, we simply couldn't. The Germans just expected us to be armed and so didn't invade, but we never fired a single gun.

Jock in the Royal Artillery (back row, second from left).

When I was stationed there, I went to a local cinema and met a girl called Morrissette who worked as the girl who took the money. We got together for a while, although her father warned her not to have anything to do with me. We would go out to the cinema, and he'd come and sit with us - just in case! At the end of the War we ended up back in Lille, and I tried to find her to see how she was, so I took a lot of flowers and went to the cinema. There was a different family who owned it but they told me that she lived about 3 miles away now. So I walked for 3 miles to find her, only to find out that she had another boyfriend in the RAF. So that was the end of that! That was my only romance until I went to Birmingham.

Then suddenly the Germans pushed through France very quickly. We were stationed at a farmhouse, and when the German push came we suddenly found ourselves being bombed. We dived for cover and waited until the bombing stopped. But when I got up again I found that the rest of my regiment had all gone. I'd been left on my own. I had no idea what was going on so I thought that I had better go to Dunkirk on my own to try to meet up with the rest of the army.

I was walking along this road when I saw a motorbike lying at the side of the road and it was full of petrol and it ran OK. So I rode this motorbike all the way from Lille to Dunkirk and then left it in a canal where a lot of other broken vehicles had been dumped. I was walking towards the beach and I saw this chap in the doorway of a house with his coat over his head. I knew he wasn't a German so I went up to see if he knew what was happening but when I took the coat off, he had no face, it had been blown off.

I walked straight down to the beach as quickly as possible. When I reached it I found the Colonel of my regiment already there. He took one look at me and said "Where've you been, White?" I had a big French overcoat on, right down to my ankles and I had a big pack full of cigarettes. When the Germans came over and bombed us on the beach we dived for cover again, and when I got up afterwards, the pack had gone. Someone had pinched it in the middle of the bombing! That was it - I wasn't thinking about the war, I was thinking about my fags.

We were lifted from the beach onto HMS Malcolm, a naval destroyer. They took us back to Southampton and from there we went back to the base where the regiment reformed and gave us new guns. They were big guns 1.15mm, much larger than the 55 pounders we had before. Then we were sent on another ship - a Dutch one, I can't remember its name - to go to the Middle East. It took us three weeks on this ship to get to Egypt. We stopped at Durban in South Africa on the way and then carried on to the desert. Rommel had pushed forward there very quickly and it looked as though we were going to be there for quite a while.

It was very very hot in the desert, and for the first six weeks I was out there I was in a real mess, trying to get used to the heat. We were all OK after that. You could simply pick up a rock and crumble it in your hands it was so dry, like salt. We had water bottles, and you would fill them up with water and dig a hole in the sand and put the bottle in it to keep the water cool. We had enough water to do our washing though, and you could dry it really easily by laying it out on the sand - it dried in no time.

It came to the night of the big barrage - El Alamein - and the guns we were using were massive with different ammunition. When we got the order to fire it must have been 1000 guns all fired at once against the Germans. The noise was deafening and it went on for 3 or 4 hours. After that, we started getting German prisoners being brought back from the front and they were all shaking the whole time because of the sheer noise. They were desperate to get away from it.

We won that battle and then we started to advance then as the Germans retreated, right through the desert to Tripoli and into Tunisia, all the way through. When we reached Tunisia, the desert war had really finished then, and we all thought that we would go home. But they ordered us back across the desert into Syria because they needed the guns again. We were given even bigger guns again - 1.55 mm American guns that we needed more training before we could use them. You could hit a target 15 miles away with one of those! We used to run up to the lines, fire everything and then get the blessed things out again as fast as possible!

Once we were trained, we were sent to Italy, to Monte Casino. That was another really big battle. The Germans were up on a hill, so close you could see them. We were all around them, but we couldn't shift them and lots of our boys were killed. We were bombing them, shelling them, but they took it all for a long time. Eventually we got them and they started to retreat. We had to follow them again, all the way up Italy into the north, fighting all the way.

When we got to the North, they said that they would take us out now, and we thought that we were going home. But no. We were shipped back to France again! I started the war at Dunkirk, and I finished it at Dunkirk! One of the guns there was hit by a German shell after Peace was declared, and two lads who had seen all the action through the war were killed.

I saw so much action and was away for the whole war, but all the time I was abroad, all I was interested in was football! The war could go hang, I just wanted to play football all the time! In fact the only time I was injured was during a game.

After the War was over we moved again, this time into Germany. We were based in a castle but didn't have much to do - we were basically waiting to go back to England. We were warned not to take anything away with you, or you would be stopped and sent back. But one of our sergeants made it back with a sewing machine and a big fur coat. I was so annoyed because I'd left all my stuff back at the castle.

When we got back to England we went back to Woolwich where I'd started my training 6 years earlier, and sat around for a few months before we were demobbed. All the Scotsmen were sent back to Scotland, so I was demobbed in Edinburgh. Then I went back to Hamilton, where I grew up, and stayed with my parents. I got a job in the steelworks, and that was hard work. I only stood it for so long, but there was no other work going so I decided to try my luck in London. I had family in Birmingham, so I thought I'd stop off and see them on the way down. When I got here, they told me there was plenty of work around and I decided to stay for a while. I worked on the buses, and that's where I met Barbara. Well, I had no chance of getting away then! I've been here 50 odd years now!

When I was on the buses, I started off as a conductor but then I learned to drive. It was better money as a driver,

A card made by Jock.

and you got five pounds up front if you passed your test. At one point I got transferred back to Scotland because we had decided to move back, but everything up there had changed so we only stayed six months before coming back to Birmingham. Then I went to Lucas factory and worked there until I retired in 1981.

Jock's medals.

That was when I started working with the Corps of Commissionaires, which I could do because I was still attached to the army. I worked all over the place and spent a lot of time at the QE hospital sports centre, booking people in and taking money. I've still got the uniform and I wear it at any events that are held here so I look like a bouncer!

Howard

I spent most of the Second World War in a labour camp in Poland as a Prisoner of War. For years I found it very difficult to talk about it, and I am only just coming to terms with what happened there.

I first joined the army when I was twenty-one at the start of conscription. You spent six months in the army and then three and a half years on the Reserve, which meant you were at home but could be called up if needed. I went into the army in July 1939, and the war broke out in September during my six months service. Nobody ever told me that my six months were now extended to the duration of the war. I just stayed in the army!

After finishing my basic training I decided I would do anything as long as it was nowhere near the front line. So I joined the Royal Army Ordinance Corps, which worked with the electrical and mechanical engineers repairing vehicles. We were sent to France as soon as the War broke out, but our station was well back from the front at a little place called Loos-en-Gohelle near Arras where some of the First World War battles had taken place. At first nothing was happening in France even though there was a war on, so we were sitting around

Howard in 1939.

with nothing to do and no vehicles to repair. It was great! Right up to the following May all we did was fraternise with the local population - a very polite way of putting it! They enjoyed having us there and we certainly enjoyed visiting!

Then suddenly the German army simply whipped through France in about a couple of days. You woke up one morning, got your bacon and eggs and Whump! The Germans were there! The only information we were given was that two or three isolated German tanks had broken through our lines. If we saw them, we were ordered to fire. There we were with half the German army in front of us, and all we had was 5 rounds of ammunition each. Someone at Head Quarters had obviously made a slight miscalculation.

On the second day after we heard the news, I saw some German tanks coming down the road. So we fired our five rounds at them and then there was nothing for us to do except turn around and march away in an orderly column. Of course, the tanks soon caught us up and we dived into the ditch at the side of the road for self-protection. I was right at the bottom of the ditch and the last to get up, unfortunately, still grasping my rifle. The German in front of us - a sergeant major type - picked up the rifle by the barrel end, swung it round and cracked it down on my head. Fortunately I had a very good steel helmet on but it was still a very unpleasant introduction to the German army.

The Germans marched us back up the road and lined us up against a brick wall. A machine gunner lay down facing us and swept his gun from side to side, checking that he could hit us all in one go. We thought that this was the end, and shook hands with the men next to us. I simply remember feeling very, very sad. But then, for some reason, they changed their minds and instead of shooting us, marched us a bit further on down the road. I don't know what happened next to the others because a few of us managed to escape by dropping out at the side of the road.

This small group of us spent some time wandering round, trying to head north towards Dunkirk, which we thought would be safer. We were really taken care of by Corporal Bob Wareham, who was in the Indian Army and a lot more experienced than the rest of us. He knew a few of the tricks of survival. He used to steal food for us and showed us how to live off leaves, where to sleep and so on - the sort of things you have to learn if you're living rough.

We were finally caught when we tried to steal some eggs from a farm which was occupied by German soldiers. We were put into cattle trucks - horseboxes that ran on the railway - with other British prisoners, about 40 of us in each wagon. Each truck had only a little ventilation hole right at the top, and we all had to go to the toilet inside it. The Germans only let us out very occasionally to give us a bit of bread and water. We were in the trucks for weeks, all the way from France to Poland.

When we reached Poland, we were put into a camp called Szubin. We were allowed to send a card home to our parents to tell them how we were, just by ticking the right box for "I am all right", "I am wounded" and so on. This was where we were first registered as Prisoners of War, so at least we had some rights under the Geneva Convention. But because we were not officers, we were put to work. People always think of Colditz and places like that when they think of Prisoners of War, but this was very different. Colditz was where the officers were held, and the Convention said that they could not be made to work at all. In their camps, they even had batmen! Non-commissioned ranks from sergeant upwards could choose whether to work or not, though often they would because you would get certain perks if you did. Everyone else had no choice. I was a private so I had to work.

Conditions in the camps were awful, but it's the details that you wouldn't really think of that made them so bad. For one thing we were lousy - we had lice all through our clothing and no change of clothing at all. What you stood up in was what you had. If you were lucky and had a pair of underpants, they would soon be too filthy to put on. There was no hot water, no heating, no soap or anything. When you went to the toilet you hadn't got any paper. And food was desperately short, there was never enough. You had stomach trouble all the time and there were people who were so ill from it that they died. When that happened, we would try to get permission to bury them, but sometimes this was denied. All these things were desperately important to us, and to people who'd been brought up reasonably decently, it was worse. You simply had to get on and deal with it, though. We had no way of getting rid of the filth and lice so we used to say that all the dirt kept us warm!

From Szubin, I was moved to a camp on the outskirts of the Polish town of Posen. There were about 900 prisoners, and we were set to farming work, digging land that hadn't been used for farming before. After the first camp, we thought the conditions were quite reasonable, though we were still frozen and starving, and the camp was very overcrowded.

I remember the first time we got Red Cross Parcels from Switzerland. We were told that they were coming, and what would be in them - milk, corned beef and all sorts of things. We talked about nothing else for days beforehand. When they arrived, the Commander of the camp made us line up in pairs because he said there was enough for one parcel between two. We didn't realise then that the Germans had taken the other half of them! We had also been told to bring a container of some sort with us, to take the contents of the parcel away. You weren't allowed to have tins, because they could be made into weapons, and you weren't allowed cardboard or paper because they could be used to make identity papers and things like that. So, the Germans removed all the paper and tin from the parcel and just poured everything into your one container - soap, condensed milk, tea, beef, everything all mixed up together. They did say they were very sorry to do that - but we knew they were laughing up their sleeves at us. All we could do was try to winkle bits out of the mess but obviously you had to eat it because you were going hungry.

It was particularly difficult to get deliveries through in an occupied country like Poland, where the Poles were the enemies of the Germans as well. People from England were sending cigarettes and clothes but they would disappear on the way and the Germans and Poles would simply blame each other for it. Whatever happened we didn't get them. I remember once I made a "Holy Smoke" out of the thin pages of a New Testament that I had with me and some raspberry leaves! I never tasted these "cigarettes" - I wasn't that daft - but I would swap them for other things that I wanted. The only things that we could have were things the Germans didn't want. We never wore pants or proper shoes or socks. Socks in the prison camps were a square of cloth that you put your foot on diagonally, turned the corners up and then slid that into wooden clogs. I used to have a Polish cavalry coat that would have gone over a horse, which was wonderful because Poland is freezing and we only had one blanket each.

The German guards treated us as though we were not even human to them. They'd hit us when they felt like hitting us, and threatened us in all sorts of ways. They made it quite clear to us that if the British won the war, we would not be alive to see it. They would shoot us if we won, and shoot us if we lost. They also told us that they had doctored the food, so that if we ever did get home, we would never have children. They made sure that the future was bleak to deliberately keep us down, you see.

In the Colditz stories, everyone seems to be escaping all the time. It was very different for us. We never had any chance at all. The camp was in a napoleonic fort. It was round with a circular courtyard in the middle and a dry moat all around the outside, so if you wanted to dig a tunnel you'd have to get down to below the moat level at least. The only place to dig from was the courtyard, so anyone trying would be spotted immediately.

Even if we made it outside the camp, we knew we would get no help from the Polish population at all. When the Germans invaded, the first thing they would do in every town was round up 10 local people, take them to the town square, and shoot them in front of everyone else as a warning. If anyone tried anything against the Germans after that, they could know what to expect. When the Prisoner of War camp was set up, the local people were told that another 10 people would be shot if anyone raised a finger to help us. And we were told that if we breathed a word of escape, we would be shot. Anyway, there was nowhere for us to run to. If you look at where Posen is on a map, you can see we were surrounded by enemies. To the north there is the Baltic Sea, and to the East, Russia, where Germany had already made great in-roads. Occupied Yugoslavia and Austria lay to the South, and Germany itself was to the West.

We also had none of the things you would need to escape. We had nothing to make false uniforms with or identity papers and so on, and we were searched whenever we left or returned to the camp. It makes sense to me that these things would have to come from outside the camps, so in places like Colditz where people did escape, the prisoners must have been swapping cigarettes with the German guards for the things they needed. Of course the Germans would be happy because they would get some decent fags rather than the rubbish they were smoking!

Looking back, I don't think anyone of us would even have been strong enough to escape. The rations at the camp were one bowl of soup a day and a fifth of a loaf of bread about six inches long and two and a half inches square. We were as thin as the people in concentration camps. When I got back to England, I was barely seven stone. There was simply no way to escape at all, so we didn't even try. You just had to live day by day, and fight to survive.

The working parties worked six or seven times a week. A lot of our work was on gas, electric and water supplies, which had been destroyed by the Poles when the Germans invaded. Often they would also have destroyed all the plans of the towns and cities. The Germans would have no record of where the pipes were, so most of the time had to build their own from scratch. That's where we came in. We would stand in a long line and, in one day, each of us had to dig a trench two metres long, one metre wide and two metres deep. By the end of that day, the Germans would have a continuous newly dug trench. Everyone who worked was given an extra bowl of soup a day.

I was ill many times during the War, but there was no point in saying you were ill because no one took any notice. The important question was could you still work. If you could, you were well. If you couldn't, you were not useful anymore. Men who couldn't work were sent to what the Germans called "hospital", and were never seen again. I had a sprained ankle once and still worked. Another time I nearly cut three of my fingers off and still worked a full day with a shovel. If anyone in the line was having difficulty, the other men would help them through. The most important thing was to carry on, to survive. It becomes a way of life. You have to hope that things will get better. If you don't accept the conditions, if you don't carry on hoping, then you die. But if you manage to live into the next minute, you've won.

I studied German at school – it's a nice language, and it was useful occasionally when we first got captured, helping the fellows understand what the Germans wanted them to do. But then one day it got me into serious trouble. We had been sent out on a last minute working party with no idea where we were going or what we were going to do. The guards took us to a train, standing in a siding, opened the wagon doors and began to throw dead bodies out of the train. I think they were Jews, or they could have been Russians or gypsies, or any of the other victims of the concentration camps. We were there to bury them. It would have been dreadful work. They must have been there for some time because the smell was awful. Worse, though, were the signs of cannibalism on some of the bodies. The group of us decided that we would not do it, and I was sent to the guards to explain, in German, that we refused to work. So I went up to the officer in charge and simply said "We're not doing this." He looked at me.

97

"Who's not doing this?" "We're not doing this." Then he pointed at me. "You're not doing this?" "Well, no, I'm not doing this but neither are the others." He shook his head and pointed again. "No," he said, "I don't care about them. Only you. And you're not doing it." And I ended up in the punishment cells for a fortnight. That was the last time that I offered to use my German!

I suppose a punishment cell in a prison camp is about as low as you can ever get. Every day you would be given a small luxury, a bowl of soup one day, half an hour outside the next day, and on the 3rd day a straw mattress to lie on, and so on. Just to show you what you were missing. The cell I remember most had one big window in it and if the sentry outside ever saw any part of you through this window, he would shoot at you. I found out that that was true one day when I got bored - for once, the Germans weren't lying.

We didn't get much outside news in the camp except for the lies the Germans fed us to keep us down. Some of the prisoners, though, were extremely clever and managed to make simple radios called crystal sets. They would make sure everyone in camp heard the small snippets of information that they received, although for the first 18 months we didn't want to hear it because it was all bad news!

In the three and a half years that I was at the camp in Posen, the only real relief came from Joyce. I clearly remember the first time I heard from her. Stupidly, I hadn't saluted a German officer, and had been thrown in the cells for 14 days. While I was in the cell, they pushed Joyce's first letter under the door for me, with a picture of her showing her knees! Cheered me up no end! She simply wrote that my mother had asked if she would like to write to me, and she had decided she would, if I didn't mind. Of course I didn't! That was the start of a correspondence that went on for four years, mainly on her side because I could only send a postcard once a month and a letter every third month. Only some of them got through and they were always checked and censored by the Germans. But we kept it going, and by the time I got home, I knew that I was going to marry her.

When the War finally started going our way, we had to leave the camp at Posen and were taken to Klimintov in Czechoslovakia. That was a really smashing place! We were set to work in a coal mine where the Germans didn't bother to shore up the ceiling you were digging under, so the more you dug the more dangerous it became. We lost quite a few fellows there, and we were only there for three weeks.

At that point, the Russians started their push against Germany. They were coming from nearby Cracow, and they were coming fast. The first we knew of it was when the Germans ordered about 200 of us to pack up everything that we had, which was not much, and then forced us to march into the Carpathian mountains, moving away from the Russian advance. The Germans were finally retreating.

That march was hard and many prisoners died on it. We did not take a direct route, but I worked it out later and we probably travelled nearly 1000 miles at roughly 20 miles a day. We marched right through January, February and March, and into April. The weather was freezing most of the time, and the altitude made it even worse. We had no provisions with us, so every time we reached a village the Germans would simply take every bit of food that they could find, and that was what we survived on. Often they did not find a lot, because the locals would hide it away when they heard we were coming. We were all seriously ill from marching so far and eating any sort of rubbish that we found just to keep us going. The Germans wanted us to move as fast as possible, and wouldn't stop for breaks; even to let you go to the toilet. Their rule was that if you had to drop out of the column, you were to be back in line by the time the last prisoners passed by, or you would be shot. Obviously, the more ill you were, the more you had to drop out, so, when you were at your weakest, you had to try to race to the front of the column before dropping out to give you more chance of making it back in time. Eventually we heard shots coming from the back of the column and I realised that some prisoners had simply decided it was easier not to bother. Men had been driven to that mental point where they preferred to die rather than carry on.

I don't know how we kept going, but eventually we finished up at a place called Ravensburg, quite a large town in Germany near Munich. The Russians were still advancing, but we had gone faster than them, so for the first time in weeks we were allowed to rest. Then the news came through that the Americans were also pushing through from the other direction. We were being held in a great big barn, and had been set to work repairing the local bomb damaged railway lines. The bombing was still going on, so often we could not work. One morning, we woke up to find that the guards had left us. We went out of the barn, and saw a line of American trucks coming towards us. The front line had passed over our heads in the middle of the night, and we were finally free.

The Americans had no idea who we were or what we were doing there, so they suggested we find the nearest British Unit. Two of us decided to turn back and make our own way home. We had just started to walk away when we heard a couple of shots, and saw two of our friends fall dead, killed by snipers up in the trees. They had both survived the prison camps for 5 years, to be killed the moment they were free.

We carried on to an American aerodrome and managed to hitch a lift to Frankfurt and then on to Rheims in France. In Rheims, we were looking around for someone to take us further when a jeep pulled up, and the British officer in the back asked us if we were Prisoners of War. We couldn't understand how he had recognised us, until he pointed out that we stunk to high heaven, were covered in lice and appeared to be wearing the same clothes we had been captured in 5 years before! We thought we looked like any other British soldiers! He still gave us a lift, though, and soon we were on a boat to England.

In all, it only took me seven days from being freed to getting home. I got to Birmingham New Street on a Sunday, and phoned the local public house to ask them to run down the road and tell my parents I would be home in half an hour. Until that call, they had no idea that I was coming back. We had a wonderful reunion, and I also met Joyce for the first time. On our first evening out, we went to the cinema to see Now Voyager. The next week we went back to see the picture!

The change from living in the camps to freedom at home came too quickly for me. I had no time to adjust to it. It was months before I could eat anything properly; I was so ill and used to such a poor diet. My Mum would cook me food that she thought I would enjoy to please me, but I just couldn't take it in. Everything that we take for granted now seemed very strange, from having a change of clothing to being able to wash to wearing proper socks and shoes.

Even after the War, I still had to stay in the army for 8 or 9 months. I had 6 weeks leave to recover, and then I was sent up to Morpeth in Northumberland for training in new weaponry that had been developed while I was a prisoner. None of us who had been in the camps were interested in the least! On the first morning, we woke up at some awful hour to the sound of some fellow blowing away on a trumpet. We looked at each other and said "What the Dickens is all this about?" And then we turned over, and went back to sleep! Of course the Commanding Officer was not too pleased that we didn't turn up on parade, but he soon realised that there was nothing he could threaten us with which was even close to being as bad as the prison camps. We were quite happy to be put in the cells for disobedience and when we found out that there was only one cell on the base, we even offered to take turns! In the end, the CO decided that anyone who was interested could be re-trained, but everyone else could forget it. So I did three weeks of absolutely nothing up there!

I was desperate to retire from the army. I worked for the clerical office during the week to serve out my time, and would spend every weekend at home with Joyce. When I could finally leave, I went back to my job at the GEC that had been held open for me from before the war, but that didn't last very long. I was selling off war equipment, and had the sense to realise that the quicker I sold it, the quicker I'd be unemployed. So I took another job as a cashier with the Birmingham Municipal Bank and studied for the student banking

The picture of Joyce sent to Howard.

exams to become an Associate of the Chartered Institute of Bankers, which I quickly passed. The bank was taken over by TSB, now Lloyds TSB. I eventually made it to district manager, with responsibility for twenty branches and nearly 200 staff. I worked there for nearly forty years, and finally retired in 1983.

I married Joyce in June 1947 in the church in Castle Bromwich. When I came back from the War I knew I was going to marry her, although I'd had another relationship before the war started. Her letters made all the difference to me - she still writes good letters, even now. We were married fifty years in 1997, so now we're looking forward to our 60th.

I haven't kept in touch with people from the camps. You got friendly with the men in your huts, but not so friendly that you wanted to see them when it was all over. I had an opportunity to re-visit Posen, but I didn't want to go. I can imagine people wanting to go back to somewhere they'd been happy, but all that going back to the camps would bring is a lot of dark thoughts, a lot of fear. If you go into a church you get a certain atmosphere, if you go into Belsen you get a different one. Its because things have happened there, and the people have left a part of themselves there, even though they have gone. There's something of me still in Posen, and that is something of me that I don't want to know.

Everything about my time in the camps is still held in my head. A couple of years ago, my daughter said that it's a pity I can't get rid of it all. But it was five

A letter to Joyce dated 28-11-1943.

years of my life - it altered me, it affects everything I have done since. I wouldn't be the same person if I hadn't gone through those years. I do find it very difficult to talk about these things even to my family. The only people I can talk to are people who've been in similar situations, and that's still very hard. I'm lucky. I still have a doorway into these memories which opens occasionally. But it always frightens me - I can't take the risk of what might happen if I leave it open, so I always try to keep it shut. I feel as if I have a barrier around me. No one can really know what it was like, and how can you tell them? It's like showing someone a television set and you don't switch on the sound, you don't switch on the picture and you tell them to look at it. A dead television set. There's simply no way that you can tell them what it was like.

I always promised myself that when I wasn't working and I had the time, I would sit down and write this story. I hoped it would help stop it running round my head. So when I retired I tried to write my memoirs, but I still couldn't bring myself to talk about the war properly. I wanted to protect my wife from the truth of it. And I didn't want my daughters to see me differently, to look at me and see someone who had been in the camps. I really did try to do it justice - sobbed my blooming' heart out over it - but I was too worried what they would think of me. My wife read it through and knew that I hadn't managed it. I finished the book, but nothing ever came of it. The substance is lacking. It's like a banana skin without the banana inside. Today, I've done it better. I've tried to be more honest about it all, but it still scares me.

In a funny way, I think that I was meant to go to the camps, to experience what I did. When I was first in France, I was told by the Commanding Officer that the army was looking for people with knowledge of German, French and Mathematics for work in the coding departments. I fitted the bill so I put my name forward and they said I would hear in a few days. Then the Germans came through France! Just a few more days and I could have been one of these people who worked on the Enigma code. Instead I spent my war in the labour camps and saw and felt things that no one who wasn't there can possibly imagine. I can't help thinking that means I have to learn from those years.

It has affected how I live my life in so many ways. There were so many good people who died there that I feel responsible - not guilty, but responsible. You cannot forget how fortunate you were to make it back, nor how fortunate we are in how we live today. People complain about petty little things all the time, but I know that you have to turn it round again and think, "No, I'm lucky". I think it's a waste of time getting angry about anything or anybody. If I haven't come to terms with the world and its anger by now then I've wasted my time.

Now, when I have any kind of meal, it hurts me to leave anything. In the camps, I used to have a dream about a cream cake factory, and my greatest nightmare was when I woke up. I still have that dream occasionally. How can you look at a picture of the people in Belsen and then say that you're hungry? You're hungry if you have no food at all, and no chance of getting any for days or weeks. You're not hungry sitting there with a kitchen full of food - you're just too blessed idle to get up and get something out of the cupboard! I've eaten raw meat. I've pushed pigs out of the way to get at their slops. I am so aware of the great need in the world today that I can't abide waste. I can't help it, not while that cream cake factory is still working in my head.

I go to church regularly now. I didn't in the camp. I'd been to Sunday school all my life, but my faith wasn't strong enough for me to believe while I was a prisoner, and I'm still coming to the point of knowing what's true. There are people who say that God was not in Belsen. I know He was, but I wouldn't like to argue that with someone who was there.

Ordinary people are not supposed to understand these things, but I can't help thinking that people who have seen more should be able to understand more. It constantly comes to me that I must learn from those 5 years. If I don't, then I've wasted them. The lower you go down - and I've been down really low - the higher you can reach up. You have to suffer to do that. Or, if you don't personally suffer, you have to accept that other people suffer and help them, through charity work and so on. If you do that, you're doing the same thing as I'm doing in trying to learn from my time in the prison camps.

Joyce

I was born in Aston and moved when I was one and a half to 150, Pelham Road in Ward End, the last house in the road at the junction of Cotterills Lane. My first memory is when I was about two and a half, and I was being wheeled about in a wooden pushchair by my eldest sister. I had a happy childhood, and I still think that we were more fortunate than children today - they may have more money and expect more things, but I think we were safer and enjoyed ourselves more.

There were five children in my family - four girls and one boy. My father worked as a toolmaker at the Metropolitan Cammel Carriage Company and was unemployed sometimes, but we never missed out at all. I was never hungry and we still had treats like fruit and cream for Sunday tea. Well, it was condensed milk, but I thought it was cream! We were all very healthy and didn't go to the doctors at all, which we would have had to pay for. The neighbours would help each other out as well. One woman who lived a couple of doors away had two children and a husband with a steady job on the trams. We always used to go round there to read their comic books. Another lady at the top of the road made toffee apples on Sunday, and we'd always get one each. You made it last for ever. You'd lick the toffee off first, until it had all gone, and only then bite into the apple. I was always sure to pick the one with the thickest toffee on the bottom as well!

I still remember the games we played when we weren't in school. We didn't have television and radio was still very scarce, so we used to play outside as much as possible. That was easy in the long summer evenings, but even in the winter we would play in front of the shops because they were lit up, so we didn't have to go in too early. We were never in any danger of being molested or attacked. Time went so quickly playing like that. My favourite games were hopscotch and wooden top, but I especially remember skipping to school. We would take the ropes off the Fyffes banana boxes and stretch them right across the road as skipping ropes. There were no cars about so we weren't in anyone's way. We would skip all the way up Pelham Road to the top of Alum Rock Road, and then all the way down Sladefield Road to the school there. We did that four times a day, because there weren't any school dinners so we had to go home at lunchtime as well.

My school was very strict. You had to do as you were told, and if you didn't you would be punished. The cane was used a lot. Some of the teachers were very nice but a lot of them would take out their feelings on the kids, so you had to watch out if they'd had a bad morning! The worst time I can remember being caned was after playtime one day. At the end of playtime, you had to stand still until the teacher told you to go into the classrooms. On this day, I was standing still when someone dropped a ball and it rolled towards me, so I simply moved my foot out to stop it rolling any further. Just for that, the teacher on duty beat me with a ruler all the way up my arm and it really hurt! She sent me back to my own classroom, and I spent the whole afternoon crying in the corner. The next day I was absolutely black and blue and I could barely move my arm. But, of course, I never moved at the end of playtime again. And it was the same at home as well. My mother was terribly strict and she would use the cane on all of us. I went to school many times with weals right up the back of my legs.

When I was in the seniors, I was head prefect of the school. That meant you could hand out punishments as well as the teachers, and were expected to keep the other children in line. We had assembly every morning from 9.00 until 9.30, and all the prefects would stand at the doors to make sure no one crept in late. Anyone who was late would be punished with a hundred lines. If children didn't hand in their lines on time, they had to see the prefects on Friday afternoon. It was set up like a court. The headmistress and 2 or 3 prefects would sit at a large table with the children in front of them, and decide how they should be further punished, either with more lines or a caning. This seemed perfectly normal at the time - you didn't question it at all, although the only reason you were doing it was because you were told to.

My favourite time of year when I was young was Christmas. We never bothered with birthday presents or even cards, but my father always made sure Christmas was special. My brother had his own room, and the girls had twin beds, but, with a couple of months to go, all five of us would get into one bed, two at the bottom, three at the top, and talk about what we wanted. We always started off with "For Christmas I would like....". My father would stand outside the door listening to all the things we were asking for. And then he would stop smoking and he'd walk to work to save money to buy our presents. He was very clever with his hands as well, and sometimes made us the toys himself. He made a lovely doll's Welsh dresser for my sister, and cots for all the girls, with drop sides and a dolly in each. On Christmas morning, we would all traipse downstairs into the main room where all the presents were piled on a table. We felt as if we were in a toyshop. It was so special because we weren't used to having much at all.

For breakfast on Christmas morning we always had an egg, and then we had beef for Christmas dinner, never turkey. My father's job on Christmas Eve was to make the pastry for the mince pies. We used to have a small Christmas tree in the window, but we couldn't have a lot of trimmings because there were real fires and lamps everywhere.

Every year, we each got a tin of toffees, and we treasured them as though they were gold. Every time you ate one, you'd count the rest to see how many were left, and it was just like counting money. For the rest of the year, you only had your Saturday penny for sweets. I'd always have a good look round in the shop to find the sweets that would last the longest, but even so they'd be finished by Sunday! Then you had to wait until Saturday came round again. I think we enjoyed that penny more than the hundreds of pounds that children get nowadays.

We celebrated other days as well that don't really get remembered now. I used to love May Day, the first of May, because all of the horses and carts were dolled up with ribbons and frills as they went on their daily business. Mothering Sunday was wonderful too. We couldn't afford cards or anything, but if you went to the sweet shop you could get special sweet bags decorated with forget-me-nots.

Although I'd passed the exam to get into secondary school, I had to leave school at 14, because my mother wanted me to start earning money. I left in the July, and a week later I started work at the Metropolitan Cammel Carriage Company, working in the office's postal department. I began work at 9.00 in the morning and sometimes didn't finish until 8.00 at night. I was paid ten shillings a week, out of which I'd keep a shilling for pocket money and give the rest to my mother. But on top of that my tram fares were paid, and for a shilling a week we were also given very good dinners in the middle of the day. If we had to work late at night, we were given toast and fish paste. I loved that. I'd never had fish paste before!

I was seventeen when war was declared. By then, we were living in Primley Avenue near Hodgehill Common. I can recall the few days previous when my mother and the next door neighbour were talking and saying how dreadful the war would be. At my tender age I thought it was all silly and stupid to worry about something that would not touch us - what a selfish attitude, but without TV I hadn't a clue what war meant. I soon found out the hard way.

The first time we were woken to an air raid was terrible. The sound of the planes overhead soon filled me with dread. We had searchlights and guns at the top of our road and the noise was shocking. Since we didn't have a shelter, at first we all crowded under the stairs. This became a regular habit until the first night the bombs dropped too close. One landed right in front of our house, and all the windows and doors were blasted in. A full curbstone was blown right over our garage and landed by the back door. That was too close for comfort. Luckily, our garden backed on to the gardens of Madison Avenue where there was a shelter, so after that night we took down a section of the fence so that we could reach it quickly. Every night my mother had blankets and flasks of tea standing ready just in case.

There was a lot of luck involved, though. A whole family of my friends was killed when their shelter was directly hit by a bomb. It was picked up and carried several streets away, with them inside it, and the shock of the blast killed them. Their house wasn't scratched. My future mother-in-law and father-in-law also had a close call. They went down the shelter one night and just as they were settling down, a bomb dropped just outside. The blast came through the door, and my mother-in-law felt it hit the side of her head. The person next to her was killed outright. A lot of people preferred to travel into the countryside at night, and sleep in their cars, but we could not do so because my eldest sister was expecting a baby. She only lived ten minutes walk away, and always came round to us during the air raids. One night, during a particularly bad raid, she went into labour. We made up her bed in the dining room downstairs and the nurse was with her all night but the doctor was delayed and he only reached us by 8.00 the next morning. It was a difficult labour, and in the end he had to use forceps. But it was lucky she was with us that night. Her house suffered a direct hit, and was completely demolished.

The Metropolitan Cammel Carriage Company, where I worked during the day, was situated next to the Saltley Gas Works, a major target for German bombers. Because of the danger, the management decided to take the office machinery downstairs into a ground floor room. A brick wall was built in front of the windows as protection against bomb blasts, so we had to work under an electric light all day. We only had a small paraffin heater, so we had to wear mittens to keep our hands warm. The smell was horrible! After a few months of this, the office was completely evacuated to a beautiful big house in Roman Road, Sutton Coldfield, Streetly. The butler and cook even stayed on to look after us! Every morning we had to report to Saltley and then travel to Streetly by Midland Red bus, which would also bring us back in the evening.

When I was eighteen, in the May of 1940, I joined the NFS (National Fire Service) on a voluntary basis along with my best friend, Connie. I would have preferred to go into the services, but my mother was set against that. She was thrilled when our office manager signed our forms to say that our work was of national importance, so we could not be called up. Connie and I started off working at the fire station that was then based at the Fox and Goose, at the junction of Alum Rock Road and Washwood Heath Road. We worked two or three nights a week and most weekends. During one of our training sessions at Ward End Park Head Quarters we were taught by the Commanding Officer, and although it sounds big headed, there was no doubt that only Connie and I knew what we were doing. Shortly afterwards, we were transferred to HQ where we stayed for the duration of the war.

Joyce and Connie.

On the nights I was on fire duty, I would rush home, have my tea, wash, change into uniform and be on duty by 7.30 in the evening. We would stay on duty until 11, when we had a hot drink and went to bed at the HQ until 6.00 in the morning. Then we would go home for breakfast and a wash down, before travelling back to the office for a full day's work. If a raid had started by eleven, we stayed on duty until it was over. We were on the phones, sending out the engines to reported fires, and taking messages about the local station stocks of engines, fire escapes and so on, in case there were any dangerous shortages. Sometimes it would be three o'clock before we got to our beds, but we were always at our office desks on time the next morning.

One weekend when I wasn't on duty, my sister and I decided to go into town. We had a few clothing coupons and needed new underwear. The tramlines had been bombed in a bad raid the night before so we had to walk most of the way into town and back. It was about 5.45 p.m. when we passed the Fox and Goose pub and turned into Brockhurst Road just past the Metropolitan Sports ground. I remember thinking it strange that a lovely sunny summer day was so quiet, with not another soul in sight. Then suddenly we heard this dreadful noise and looking up over to our right, saw a German bomber coming so close that we could see the insignia. We had nowhere to shelter. My sister just froze. I tried pulling her, but she couldn't move with fear. After what seemed an age, I managed to get her legs going and we ran towards home. Before we got to Madison Avenue, the sirens started. We raced down Primley Avenue towards our house, and saw our mother standing in the front doorway desperately looking out for us. She had us down the shelter quick as a flash.

The wonderful thing I can remember of those dark days was the feeling of joy each day when I met my friends again and knew that they were alive and safe. I still wake up in the early hours and, if it is moonlight, I smell those nights again, and feel the fear in my stomach. I hope and pray my children and grandchildren will never know the fear of cowering in a hole in the ground while you listen to the whistle of the bombs falling. We always said that you don't hear the one that gets you. At the time, that was no help.

I first met Howard's family through Connie, who was married to his brother. He was serving overseas, and Connie asked me to call at the house to see if there was any mail from him. I liked "Mum Powell" as soon as I met her, and after that one visit she asked me to write to Howard in the prison camp. For six months after he went missing, she didn't know whether he was alive or dead. That must have been very hard. Then one day she was walking up Alum Rock road and saw him coming down the road. She took it as a sign that she was going to hear something about him soon, and the very next day she received the postcard telling them that he was a prisoner of war. I agreed to write to him, and sent letters as often as I could, though many of them went astray. I also sent cigarettes to him, but he never received them. Maybe someone in Poland or Germany enjoyed them. It was shame because my money was scarce. Taxes in the war were very high, and half of your wages were taken away before you saw them.

I first met Howard on the day that the war in Europe ended. I was out with a friend, and my mother came to meet us at the cinema to tell us that the war was over. We didn't know whether the next day would be a holiday or not, so I went round to Connie to see whether we had to go to work or not. What I didn't know was that Connie was out for a walk with Howard, so we ended up meeting by chance in the street. That was very awkward, especially because I wasn't dressed up at all! I kept my back towards him a little bit and barely spoke to him! I made up for it next morning, though. I went round again to tell them it was a holiday, but this time I was dressed up to the nines!

Howard found it very difficult coming home again. Living like that for five years - it's a terribly long time to not know whether you are going to see home again. And it only took him a week to get back. He told me later that on the day he finally came home he got off the bus several stops early because he knew his parents would be looking out for him and he needed more time to get used to the idea. The first time we went out together, we went to the cinema, but I couldn't watch the film knowing that he was next to me, and we couldn't talk together either. Afterwards, though, we walked for miles and miles, talking. I know he kept a lot of the really awful things to himself, but he told me quite a bit about the camps. I think a lot of pain came out in those first months. He says now that he never remembered talking about it. It must have taken him years to really settle down. He couldn't hold a proper meal down for a couple of years. But the only time I really saw it come back to him was when my daughter found the cards and letters he had sent to me and asked me to read them to her. It broke his heart. I think he could see himself writing them, you see, and he didn't want to go back there. There is so much still locked inside him and I don't know that it will ever come out now.

My mother didn't want me to marry Howard at first. I had been seeing an American boy, from California, and she thought I should marry him. That was one of the few times I ever held out against my mother. Even after I was married, and right up until she died, she had the final say in my life. But I knew that Howard was the right one for me. I didn't want to be up-rooted from my whole family and country to live with someone I really knew very little about. What do you do then, if he wasn't the right one for you? I was lucky to meet Howard when I did, otherwise I would probably have married my American and only found out that it wasn't the right thing to do later. I can understand why divorces happen, now. Howard was so calm about the whole thing, even though I was arguing with my mother over it for years. I was right, though. We've been really, really happy all these years.

When we first married, we lived with Howard's parents for a while, though we both wanted a home of our own. Then we moved in with a couple of friends of ours for a while. They'd bought a house, and let us have rooms there to help them with the mortgage. They had the front room, we had the back room and we shared the kitchen but we got on so well that there was no problem.

Our first real home was a bank flat in Bordesley Green that Howard got through his banking job. We stayed there for about four years, until we managed to get another one at Hall Green which was bigger. It was actually very difficult to get a mortgage when you were employed by the bank, because they took the view that the money was for the customers, not the staff, so we were lucky to get the bank accommodation. We couldn't really afford things like decent carpets at first, or fridges or washing machines, but we saved up for them, and when we finally got them, I thought it was the most wonderful thing! And the flat was lovely. It had three bedrooms, with a massive kitchen. We made one of the bedrooms into a dining room and the two girls had twin beds in their bedroom. There were no neighbours, so we could have parties whenever we liked. In the end, we were there for about forty years.

The bank was taken over by TSB and they decided to close a lot of branches including Hall Green, so that we were living above an empty building for about eight years. We were very vulnerable there. The garden was so long that we were getting trouble with children coming into it. Fifty years after Howard came home from prison camp, we put barbed wire round our garden. He said "I've come out of barbed wire, and now I'm going back into barbed wire". It really got to him. So we decided to move out, and we came to Brook Meadow Court about five years ago.

We absolutely love it here. I think everyone living on their own would be much happier in a home because you've got so many friends close by. The people here are now part of my family and every time someone is ill, or passes on, it feels like it's one of your family going. There's something going on every night here - Bingo 3 nights a week, cards 2 nights a week, and next year we're going to have a lot of Saturday activities because that tends to be the night that people get bored. We had Christmas dinner last Thursday, but a lot of people go away to their families for Christmas so we don't do much else except for Christmas drinks on the night itself.

We see our children and grandchildren quite a lot, though not so much now that we can't travel. My one daughter lives in Wimbledon, and the other lives in Broseley in Shropshire, and we have five grandchildren, three girls and two boys. They all came along at once after Howard retired. There is a woman here with 46 grandchildren! I'm glad I haven't got that many - I really don't think I could keep track of them!

Margaret

I've always lived in Birmingham. I was born in 1923, which makes me seventy seven now. There were three children in the family. My Mum had had two boys and wanted a girl, so when I arrived my Dad put the flag out! I was always my Dad's favourite. I had a very good childhood and I always think I was lucky because every year we went away on holiday. We used to take the last two weeks in August, because then the school holiday was only a month and Dad wouldn't let us be away from school. We used to go to Scarborough and Bournemouth, and just before the War we went to Jersey as well.

I was about eighteen when the Second World War began. I was working in the wages office at Dennison's, who made watch cases and powder compacts. I wanted to join the forces, but my Dad wouldn't let me go. He said, "Your place is at home with your mother!"

So instead I joined the Red Cross. I was trained in the basics at Night School, but I wasn't allowed to do any real nursing. Once a week two of us manned the mobile canteen at New Street station from ten until four in the morning, when the troop trains came in with soldiers coming home on leave. That was a long night, and then we'd run back home to change and do a full day's work as well. We also helped out at Highcroft Hall, which is over Erdington way, with the doodle bomb patients who had come up from London. Friends of mine were also in the Land Army and the Fire Service. Anytime any one of us went into the forces, Mum would have a photograph taken and she kept them lined up on her sideboard. She used to call it the Rogues Gallery!

My two brothers were in the Territorials and got called up at once. Dennis, the middle one, was a metallurgical chemist which was a reserved occupation, so he had to come back after only six weeks. He tried his utmost to get back into the army because all his friends had gone to war, and he was stuck at home. They wouldn't release him at all, so he joined the Home Guard when that was formed. He got married as well, and set up home with his wife. My oldest brother, Jack, was at the invasion at Dunkirk in 1940. He was in England then for two years doing officer training, and then he went out to India as a lieutenant. He ended up as a major in Bangkok. We never saw him in his officer's uniform, though. He only came home after he was demobbed in 1946.

Margaret in her Red Cross Uniform with her friends Betty and Edna.

You couldn't have much of a holiday during the war, so some of us went "on the land" for two weeks. Picking fruit and digging vegetables, that kind of thing. It may not sound like much of a holiday, but it was fun, although the first year we went, we were under canvas, and I didn't like that much. We did get nights off. One time, they took us all on a lorry to Stratford, but because we'd been out in the fresh air all day, everyone fell asleep watching Othello!

I first met my husband Bill in 1954 in Guernsey, where we stayed in the same hotel. He lived in London where he worked at the shipping office of Wimpeys in Hammersmith. He only lived in a bed-sit so, if I went down to London, he would book me into the Bedford Hotel. When he came to see me, he could stay in my Mum's house. We were both fond of classical music, so he would always book a show when I went down, and I would book seats at the Town Hall. The journeys were difficult though. He would catch the last bus to New Street and then get the train to London, waking up all the squaddies who were asleep on the seats so that he could sit down! Then he had to walk from the station a long way to where he lived. He gave up drinking and smoking to afford the fare. He wasn't fond of Birmingham; the first time he came up, he thought it looked like a cemetery lit up! And he was a Chelsea supporter - he followed them all round the country. But it was silly for him to travel up all the time, so he got a transfer to the print room at Wimpeys on the Chester Road, producing plans for the architects. We got married at the little church on School Road in Yardley Wood and went back to Guernsey on our honeymoon, to the hotel where we first met.

My son, Stephen, was born on 19th February 1960 - the same day as Prince Andrew. A shop in Kings Heath gave a free Ladybird sleeping bag to any baby born locally on that day, but my Mum had to go and fetch ours because I was still in hospital. My husband always thought I had something in common with the Royals. My surname is Bonham, you see, and I used to get called Lady Margaret all the time!

I was a long time in labour and had to have a Caesarean in the end, but the lack of oxygen to Stephen's brain caused spasticity on his left side. He can't feed or look after himself at all, and he is really a dead weight to carry around. Bill was a wonderful husband to me, and would do anything for Stephen. Unfortunately, he developed bad diabetes very soon afterwards, and the doctors thought it was the shock of Stephen's birth that caused it. But we did accept the situation in the first place - I think that's where a lot of people go wrong in not wanting to accept it. We may have had a lot of heartache, but we also had a lot of fun!

When he was a baby, we would take him out in his pram, but he soon outgrew that. He couldn't hold his head erect enough to sit in a wheelchair safely, so we got a spinal carriage instead. It was huge! Bill had to take a bit off the back gate to turn it, and once it was in our hall it couldn't go any further. Any visitors had to go round the back because no one could get in through the front door. When I was pushing it, Bill had to be at the front doing hand signals, and you could see cars slowing down to watch us go past! Mind you, it was ideal because you could get all your shopping in it!

After a year, he was strong enough to have a wheelchair. But then he needed an operation on his left foot which had dropped through not using it. The doctor cut the tendons at the back of his leg and put him in plaster to straighten the foot. His leg had to be kept up in the air for a while but the wheelchair didn't have a proper support, so my brother Dennis made one from half a drainpipe! Stephen also had to wear a big shoe that held his foot in place in bed. The only trouble was the sole of the shoe was metal, so I had to wrap it in old sheets every night, to stop his moving around in bed from wearing my sheets out! But it worked, and once the plaster came off he could get better shoes on. At first we had to buy split size shoes from a shop, but eventually the Children's Hospital made them for him.

Stephen couldn't do a lot as a child, but he liked music and he loved having people around him. I used to take him to the shops to see the lights and people. We took him to the Isle of Wight, as well, and to Paignton, Bournemouth and Weston. A friend of Bill's who lived in Essex used to come up about twice a year and take Stephen out. He filmed him too, and I had it put onto video.

Our biggest problem was bathing him because he was so heavy. We complained about it, so two nurses came round to see if we could do it any better. They were hopeless! When Bill got the water ready, one of them asked him if he'd tested it with his elbow. Bill was livid. He'd been doing it for sixteen years, after all! When she saw us lifting him in and out of the bath, she said "What about your back, what about your back!" But he had to come out some how! When they went, she said "I must say, you do keep him spotlessly clean. We can't improve on what you're doing." And that was that. I thought, if I'd been a nurse, I'd have been ashamed to admit that they couldn't help us. Some time after that, we got a sunflower bath, which fitted over our bath so you didn't have to bend as low. But it wouldn't go over our taps, which were on the bath side, so the only way we could fill it was with the hose from the washing machine attached to the wash basin! It made a bit of difference, though.

When he was older, Stephen went to a Day centre while Bill was at work, to give me some time to tidy up and do the washing. Then, when he was 19, I had to go into Queen Elizabeth hospital with a thrombosis, and Stephen went into a home while I was away. I suggested to Bill that we make the break then. We knew it would have to come sooner or later. We couldn't have managed much longer, anyway, and if we didn't make the break then, we could have to wait ages for a vacancy. So Stephen went to Moneyhul.

At first, he had to share his room, but then they built these bungalow's that he's in now. They are lovely - I could live in one myself. They've got a bath that goes up and down so you can get in easily, and you can make it a Jacuzzi or a whirlpool just by pressing a button. And there's a special hoist with a track across the ceiling so that you can get from your bed to your chair. There are 5 other patients, in the bungalow, but Stephen's got his own room and the carers are always there to help. They're so good to him.

Margaret and Stephen.

They took him to Tenerife, and I've got pictures of him in the pool at the hotel. He was 40 this year and they had a party for him with a cake shaped like a dog and everything.

I've been at Brook Meadow Court for fifteen years - I was one of the original inmates! It hasn't really changed a lot except for the people. Stephen comes over for lunch every couple of months, and I go every week to see him. The home is only about three miles away, and when I visit, they pick me up in their own minibus and take me there. He's made a lot of progress since he's been there because they are trying to get him to walk. There's one unit for occupational therapy, and they've got a snooze room full of lights and padded walls with different touches - hard, soft, hot or cold - and he really loves it. Just the other week he took seven steps, with the physiotherapist holding him up.

A recent photo of Stephen.

Una L

He was at a theatre in Manchester. Mother took me there when I was about three weeks old, and at that time, you know Colonel Cody, they used to call him Buffalo Bill, had brought his Wild West Show to Manchester. As you know, different Companies always send out invitations to each other, and Buffalo Bill had sent out an invitation for Father and Mother to go and see his show. Mother had to take me, and as we were getting towards the tent, Buffalo Bill came along the pathway and met Mother. He said, "Oh, you've brought your little one. Do let me hold her."

He took me and he carried me all around the big tent, and put me in the arms of the Big Chief Indian, Sitting Bull. He was thrilled to death, saying, "Little Porpuss, little Porpuss". After we'd seen the show we came out and Buffalo Bill followed us, and he said, "Mrs. Moseley, what are you going to call your little one?"

Mother said, "Well, I haven't named her yet".

He said, "Would you let me give her a name?

He said, "I should be thrilled".

So he said, "Would you let me name her Una. She was a favourite niece of mine, who had an accident and died. It would please me so much if I had someone else called Una". And that was how I got my name.

We've all belonged to the theatrical profession. When my father was quite young he joined an operatic company in Yarmouth. From that time he was in it for years, right up to the time he went blind. I'm also blind now, but we've had a very interesting life. I've travelled very near all over England and abroad as well. My dad would always take us with him, wherever he went. My sisters and I used to go with them, and we've met some very interesting people.

When I was about four years old, we went from Wales to Scotland. We went to Willie Fife, the Scots comedian. His father had got what we used to call the fit up theatre, a portable theatre. We joined his father, and he was a huge great big man. He was a proper Scotsman. He'd take me on his knee, he used to have a pony trap, and he used to take me by his side for miles and miles. I used to love it. I used to think he was a King, or something like that.

He used to teach the children. I remember we used to have a pantomime there, it was Cinderella. He was trying to teach the younger ones for the chorus and that sort of thing. He got me to sing a little song, and it was 'The Boo Peep'. I used to hide behind a chair.

From that we went on and on, and we'd go to different companies. We met Stanley Holloway. He was in the same company, and lots of other people. We had a very happy life until father lost his sight.

After that he didn't want me to go back. I used to do a bit of dramatic business at the last theatre I was at, which was Plymouth Theatre Royal. When Father died, he made me and Ivy promise that we wouldn't continue with it, as he didn't care for us to go alone. So we had to give that up.

My eldest sister, Vera, she did keep in it all her life until she died (Vera was a Ballet Dancer). Ivy and I had to learn to do something else. In our lifetime we've practically done everything under the sun, to bring in a living, because father had got his little house in Bromyard in Herefordshire. We stayed there for

Una's husband Albert.

seventeen years. During that time I've learned farming, helping little pigs into the world. I've done nursing. I nursed a very bad case of cancer, and I had a breakdown.

We had to move to Birmingham. They asked me to come up for the holiday. I did in September 1924, and I've never been away again, because the first road I came into I met my husband, Albert. A very lovely pianist and he came to play at a party Mr. Allen was giving me. We got together, and he said, "Are you obliged to go back home again, Una?"

I said, "No I needn't go back, but I need to find some living to do".

He said, "What do you do?"

I said, "Anything, I don't care what I do".

Later on he said, "You wouldn't mind being a barmaid would you?"

I said, "Yes, if it keeps me here". So I went as a barmaid to a public house called "The Golden Cross" in Aston. I was there

Albert and Una on their wedding day.

for three months, and Albert came one night and he said, "Come on, get your coat on, you're not stopping here any longer", and away he took me.

Then I got a very nice place as a companion to a lady in Sutton Coldfield. I was there, really, until I married. From then, of course, it's all been up and down, up and down, all through the War. I've got this big house, I'm still in now. I've been here fifty-three years, and I can tell you no end of stories about the different families and people and boys I had here during the War. I had over twenty men to look after and cater for. I can't say I've had an unhappy life, and so I've got to be contented now, and try and settle down, which I know I'll never do, I know!

I've got a lovely daughter (*Una W.*). She's been okay to me all her life. She's been a proper companion as well as a daughter, and I'm in the care of some very good friends. My daughter had twelve children. I've got eleven grandchildren now, and twenty-four great grandchildren. They all come to see me every now and then. I'm very pleased to see them. I've also got a very good friend, who came as a boarder to me twenty-six years ago, and he's still with me. He's looking after me now, which since I've lost my sight, I can't do a lot. I'm not sixteen any longer, am I? Without him I don't know what I should do, but for all that, I think he'll look after me all right.

My married name was Lissimore. I married Albert Lissimore. We live in Erdington now. I have what they call the Sutton newspaper that they let the blind have every week. I would like to let them know and to thank them, for all the news and little parties that they've given to us. We have quite a lot of nice outings, belonging to the Blind Institute, and I still like to go out with them. I don't like to say what I've got, but I've got arthritis from my ankles right up to my neck.

But I must shut up now. I could go on talking forever! Bye bye for now.

Una W

I was born in Loveday Street, Birmingham at the Old General Hospital in 1927. I was the only child of Albert and Una Lissimore. An early memory of my father is that he would take me to a show to see young ballet dancers.

My first school was Osborne Road Erdington, but I was only there for a week as the teacher found out that I couldn't read the blackboard. I was short-sighted, so I was taken to Whitehead Road Aston School, a school for the partly blind. There were only three classrooms, a small kitchen and a bathroom where we were given a bath every week. I was very small and the big children made a fuss of me.

My father died when I was eight years old. My grandmother and auntie also lived with us. It was a three-storey house at 10b Wood End Road, Erdington. It had five bedrooms with a kitchen. After my father died my mother took in boarders to help with the budget. She had fourteen at one time, many of them foreign gentlemen. She had them all through the war. She also fostered five children - three boys and two girls.

I would go to my other grandmother and grandfather's house every Sunday and take my cousin Sheila out to the park. I was about six years older than she was. We walked around Brookvale Park and fed the ducks on the pond. I don't remember any more events from my childhood until I was about fourteen.

My mother got me my first job, which was at Taylor's in Erdington. It was a store which sold almost everything. We had to wear black dresses, but as Mom couldn't afford a black one, the next best thing was a navy dress, which was cheaper. I was put on the wool counter. It was sold skeins, not in balls of wool, measured in ounces. The money would be put into a small cylinder, with the bill. It would travel across the ceiling to a small office, where the lady would send down the change.

After that job, I went to work in a children's nursery in Coleshill Road, Washwood Heath. The matron and sister were very strict, but I enjoyed it there for three years. The mothers would bring their children in the early morning and go and work in the ammunitions factories all day. We also looked after the babies all night. I used to work from seven in the evening until seven in the morning.

While I was there I met my husband, Vic. Vic was a soldier and I met him through a bet. I was going to the Palace Picture House that day. It was 1945. As I approached, four of his friends said, "the first girl who comes down the road, you will make a date with her". Of course, it was me. Vic paid for me to go into the pictures. I loved going to the pictures and we had a lovely time. I would go twice a day on Sundays, from one to the other straight afterwards. There would be two films and the news. In the afternoon, after seeing 'Gone with the Wind' Vic took me home to meet his parents at 66 Alleyne Road, near the Tyburn Road. He was to go back to camp that night, so I went to the train station at Snow Hill with him. From that time I would meet him from the station every Saturday. We were very happy together.

While Vic was away I was busy working nights at the nursery. I would go to work on a bike and get home to Mom's house about 7:30 a.m.

I had met Vic in October 1945, got engaged in February 1946 and got married in May 1946. We were married at the Registry Office in Edmund Street. There were only five of us; Vic and me, Vic's Dad and two of my Mum's lodgers as witnesses. I wore a little grey second hand suit with a pink and black ribbon on which I trimmed myself. I had a new pair of pink French knickers. The nightdress was so long and thin, like a parachute. In fact, it was made from a yellow parachute. I'm not quite sure what happened to it!

Whitehead Road School, Una third from left, middle row.

After the ceremony, we went for a drink at the little pub nearby. We didn't stay and went back to my Mom's house for a bit of tea. Mum had made us a little cake and sandwiches. We lived in the front room downstairs, and a bedroom in the kitchen, while Mom, Auntie and Gran lived upstairs. We only had three days together as Vic had to go back to camp.

One week Vic took me to Thatcham, as he was on duty there. He knew a lady who put me up for a week. It was a lovely little country place and very small. But after a week, Vic put me on a train for home.

Una with her children on her 65th Birthday - left to right. Una (Junior), Cindy, Victor, Tina, Marie, John, Penny, Edwin, Peter, Emma, Anthony.

I had a job in Woolworth's before I was married, working on the biscuit counter. We had to weigh the biscuits, wrap them up and take the food coupons as well as adding up the contents.

After getting married, I got another job in Littlewoods in Erdington, but I didn't stay very long as I was pregnant. Vic came into the shop one day and said I was finishing there. He told the manager I was leaving. I was about four months pregnant.

Vic soon went to Egypt for a year. While he was away my eldest son John was born, on May 17th 1947. He was six months old when Vic came home on embarkation leave and it wasn't long before he was de-mobbed from the Army.

I had a second baby Marie in 1949 and we were still living at Mum's house. Edwin was born in 1951. I was listening to the radio when I was in labour, when 'Sugar Ray Robinson' won a title fight.

When Edwin was a month old, my Grandmother died and we left soon after for our first house, which was number 11 Sheep Street, Gosta Green, Birmingham. It had one small living room and a small kitchen, which contained a small cooker and a sink. It had two bedrooms, one on top of the other. It had a black grate, which I polished and a red stone floor that I cleaned two or three times a week with red polish. There was a cellar where the coal and coke was put in by the coal man. But if we were short of money, I used to go with the pram to fetch it from the coal yard. There would be at least four children hanging on the pram. They loved to go to the market with their comics and change them. If they had six, they could get three back.

We lived next door to a small grocer's shop. Mrs. Jones wasn't very friendly and she would only let me have one pound ten shillings worth of food a week 'on tick', as she said, I couldn't afford any more. But we had good neighbours in our small house. You could leave your doors open all day and night without any fear of intruders.

By this time I had five more children and Vic had a job just across the road at Southalls. He drove their lorries with their merchandise to different shops.

The children went to Bishop Ryder's School. They had baths there as we didn't have a bathroom. We had to share a toilet outside with two other families. I did the washing in the brewhouse at the top of the yard, and the children would play in the old air raid shelter. We didn't have a television until 1953. We lived in this little house until 1962, until we moved to Allens Croft Road, Kings Heath.

It was much larger, with two front rooms, a small kitchen, a bathroom, three bedrooms and there was a nice front garden and one at the back. It was quite pleasant.

Our eldest son, John, got a job on a farm. He was away from home. He loved it there, but when he finished, he got a job in a small hardware shop at the top of the road. In 1967 John was killed on his motorbike in Allens Croft Road at the top of the hill, near where he used to work.

We left in 1976 for Ithon Grove, Kings Norton and we had four more children in this house - Victor, Penny, Emma, and our youngest son, John. The house was much bigger, as it had four bedrooms and a toilet downstairs, and the living room was upstairs with a bathroom and toilet.

Most of the older children had left to get married. Victor and John went to Primrose School, just down the road from where we lived. Penny and Emma went to Dame Elizabeth Cadbury's in Bournville. We stayed there until 1989, when we moved to Baldwin Road, Kings Norton.

We were there for only three months when my husband, Vic, died of heart disease. I stayed on for a year with John and Clare, who was John's girlfriend at the time.

I got my first voluntary job at Oxfam, in Northfield, sorting bags and working on the till. I had put my name down for a bungalow, which I got in 1990. It was 31 Hawkesley End, Kings Norton. Before I moved in John and Clare moved to another flat.

After a time I got my second voluntary job at the Children's Hospice in Cotteridge. I left OXFAM to concentrate more on the shop at Cotteridge, and I was there for three years.

I also started a new voluntary job on 6th March 1993, at Selly Oak Hospital on the Rheumatology ward. I helped make the tea for the staff and patients, water the plants and lay clean green paper on the beds, to keep the beds clean when people lay on them. I enjoyed my work there. I didn't stay very long there, as it was too long a journey to get there. I also gave up the bungalow as I was broken into three times in six months. I was there four years and left in 1995.

The next flat I was given was in Hall Green. It was a nice place, but so cold. I started work in Age Concern in Kings Heath. I like it very much. I have been there now five years.

I put in for a Sheltered Home in Hall Green. I'm in Brook Meadow Court now. I have plenty of friends here, and I love it. My children come up on Sundays, with their children. I had six boys and six girls, and I've got forty-five grandchildren and nineteen great grandchildren. I am very happy now.

6. STUDENT VIEWS

What we enjoyed

"My favourite bit was learning about the old spinning tops and games they used."

"Talking to old people and finding out about them."

"They said when they were little, if they were late, which they probably weren't ever, they would get told off and have the cane, or have another punishment, which were all quite scary!"

"You get to ask people questions, know about what kind of lives they had, what happened, fascinating."

"What it was like in school then."

"When I got to see their games or curlers, and we got to try them out."

"I've enjoyed it a lot. I especially liked when we first met the old people and we were handing out refreshments. David showed me all the trams."

"I think they enjoyed it too. Some of them might, or might not have grandchildren. They might never talk to children."

"When we go into the homes of the elderly people. When they went to war, and what kind of houses they had."

"Their first jobs they had and how the transport was different."

"Margaret and her sewing."

"Their homes were back to back."

"When we go into the homes of the elderly people. When they went to war, and what kind of houses they had."

"I liked everything. I liked the games."

Good Practice Award

Presented to

Billesley Cadbury Time Children's Club

For Outstanding Achievement Of Your Club In The Following Areas:

☺ Activities Created For & By The Children

☺ Activities That Are In Line With Play Values

☺ Activities That Are Fun!

Signed: ..Valerie Ottens.., BPCN Chair
(On Behalf of the Board of Trustees)

Date: ...9th June 2003....

Award presented to Billesley Primary School for the AGElink project from Birmingham Playcare Network.

Living history captured for new generations

Youngsters from Birmingham schools enjoyed a lesson in living history as they captured the memories of an older generation.

Wartime tales and childhood games were some of the memories captured by children in their conversations with their elders for the Birmingham Lives project.

The children, from Billesley Primary School, Shenley Court Technology College, Baverstock School and Dame Elizabeth Cadbury Technology College, used video, photography, voice recordings and art and crafts to record the reflections of the pensioners.

The community project, which had secured a £14,000 grant from the Countryside Agency's Local Heritage Initiative, brought together schoolchildren aged eight to 17 with older people from local care homes, to talk about their lives.

The recordings, currently on display at Birmingham's Central Library, will be kept for the next 200 years in Birmingham's archives.

Birmingham historian Chris Upton, who opened an exhibition of the project at the library yesterday, said the recordings provided a valuable insight into how people once lived in the city.

He said: "Oral history is important, most of history is walking around on two legs and we don't ask enough about it. There is no better way to find out about history than talking to people who have lived through it. But in addition it has put two generations together and got them talking."

Liz Collins, community officer at Billesley Primary School, said: "The children found it very rewarding and they got such a lot out of it. It is all about bridging the gap between the young and old."

Among the children interviewing the pensioners was 11-year-old Tasha Beck from Billesley Primary School.

She said: "We talked to older people about how their lives were when they were younger. I found out that when they used to go to school if they were naughty they would get caned.

"It is a really great project because now we can tell everyone about other people and how they lived."

Her twin sister Tanya added: "I was a bit scared at first but they were really nice. One lady showed me how to sew."

Fellow pupil ten-year-old Townsend Forbes said: "I talked to them about old toys like spinning tops. We also talked about the war. It is very important because I like old things and things to do with the old days like the Second World War."

Elsie Levi, aged 80, of Kings Heath, said it was vital elderly shared their memories with younger generations.

"I think we didn't ask our elders enough about life when they were growing up and when they die we are left dangling with many unanswered questions."

Birmingham Post July 26th 2003.

106 happy returns

GOLDEN oldie George Rice may turn 106 today but he is still set to liven up the party with his musical talents.

George will delight the Lord Mayor of Birmingham, fellow residents and staff at his home in Tandy Court, Tandy Drive, Kings Heath, with a short rendition on the mouth organ and keyboard. George, a former metal worker at Rover's Longbridge plant, is very musical and has been playing instruments since he was 10-years-old. City mayor, Coun John Alden, is dropping in to mark George's 106th birthday with tea and cakes while a guitarist and singer take over the entertainment.

The Lord Mayor said: "It is marvellous to see George reach his 106th Birthday and find out the secret of his longevity."

George was born in Stockton-on-Tees and was awarded the Legion D'Honneur medal in 1999 for his service during the First World War.

■ *MAKING MUSIC: George Rice*

Birmingham Mail, 18th June 2002.

From left, Elsie Levi from Kings Heath, Townsend Forbes, aged ten, from Billesley Primary and Barry Levi at the Agelink Exhibition

Birmingham Post July 26th 2003.